Therapeutic Channelling

SEAN BRADLEY

This book has been printed digitally and produced in a standard specification in order to ensure its continuing availability

Published by Antony Rowe Publishing Services in 2005
2 Whittle Drive
Highfield Industrial Estate
Eastbourne
East Sussex
BN23 6QT
England

ISBN 1-905200-16-1

Printed and bound by Antony Rowe Ltd, Eastbourne

Therapeutic Channelling for Practitioners

Therapeutic Channelling for Practitioners is the long-awaited sequel to Sean Bradley's bestselling book ***Angelic Energies.***

Behold –Enfold –Hold –Listen to your heart centre, your teacher, connecting you with Source –with Christ – with The Four Spheres of Angels.

The book is aimed at experienced therapists and healers, and everyone who is interested in spiritual development and self-healing. Sean Bradley draws upon his 38 years of caring for the sick/dying and teaching experience to provide step-by-step advice and guidance on working in a closer partnership with the Christ /Angelic healing energies, empowering you to take back your personal power and reclaim your inner child –your teacher. This book encompasses all energy.

Therapeutic Channelling of the Christ /angelic healing energies engenders unconditional love creating harmony, balance and a true connection with all that you truly are as a co-creator of Source.

Praise for your Healing Power:

I was at your workshop yesterday in Dublin; it was so beautiful for me. I felt truth more than anything else, the love was pure but the words were so real and alive in all that you expressed. It left me in no doubt that I am an angel of God and that I can make the world a better place. I am delighted I got to spend a day in your lovely Divine presence; I deeply respect your journey; your truth. God must be so proud of you & the courage you show each day. I am blessed by your example & our meeting will be cherished & revisited in my Soul again. **Namaste, Gillian (Dublin).**

Audio Recordings by Sean

Create Your own Personal Angel Peace Garden
Come & Explore the Wonder of Angels ***The Angel Teaching Series Collection. : Double CD***
Embracing Your Inner Essence **(Practitioner Heal Thyself)**
Your Wounded Child is Your Teacher
Communicating with Angels
Heal yourself with the Christ Energy
Angel Healing Series (4 healing meditations – Double CD)
Heal Yourself with Angelic Love & Light
Four Seasons Healing Meditation
Relaxation Healing Series Healing **Meditations**
Relaxation Healing Series Healing Meditations
Walking with Angels
Angel Healing Day Souvenir CD
Therapeutic Channelling Video
Festival of Angels Manchester
The Barefoot Angel Man-This film shows Sean, in action, at one of his many successful workshops at his home in Storth, Cumbria; held in the beautiful surroundings of Chapel Gap. He takes the four students attending the Beginner's course in Therapeutic Channelling through 2 meditations
Celebrating Christ's Energy for 2012 (DVD/Video)

The above recordings can now be purchased on-line by visiting Sean's website www.sean-bradley.com

Books by Sean

Angelic Energies

Let Your Divine Light Shine

Reflections & meditations for your Angel peace Garden.

Through Trauma we are Re-Born (Sean's life story)

E -Books by Sean

Create An Oasis for Angels

Sacred Planting Designs for an Angel peace Garden.

Sacred Tools for Divine Angel connectedness in your Angel Peace Garden.

Four Seasons Healing Meditation Through Trauma we are re-Born

Channelling the Christ Energies

Therapeutic Channelling for Beginners

Contents

Wrap yourselves in humility to be servants of each other,
Because God refuses the proud
and will always favour the humble.

Bow down, then, before the power of God now,
and he will raise you up on the appointed day;
unload all your worries on to him,
since he is looking after you.
1 Peter 5: 5b-7

Dedication

I dedicate this book to my Heavenly Father and my Earthly Mother, to my spiritual teachers, the Lord Jesus, Saint Mary Magdalene, Mother Mary, St Francis, all the Archangels and healing angels, my guardian angel and all spirit guides who have supported me with this book.

To my 'earthly teachers' who are my student therapists, therapists and the teachers of the Academy. They are, (Ireland), Bernie, Angela K, Margaret, Caroline K and Caroline R. In the (UK), Jeanne, Sue, Anthony, Carol R, Angela S, Aggie, Vivien, Helen, Helen R, Theresa, Cindy, Janet, Sue, Jeanette, Angela A, Paula. Martin, Athena, and Mum in Bulgaria.

To Graca, Angela, Rosario and the many light workers whom I met in beautiful Madeira and who gave me a beautiful message from the Archangel Michael empowering me to carry on the 'Good Fight' in the name of Love.

Thank you for being my teacher and empowering me to fly home to the light of God's love.

Dedicated to Sean.

The Barefoot Angel Man

Sean you are a man of faith,
Sean your life is blessed with grace.
A man so talented pure and free,
You showed us love and said, "Just be".
Chapel Gap is an energy portal;
You taught us we are more than mortal.
We are spirit shining like the stars,
We can travel anywhere and we don't need cars.

You are surrounded by love, Rob, Winston and Miss Elle,
With all that love who needs the telly.
The house is filled with peace and love,
The garden is blessed by the angels above.
We came to you as limping wrecks,
You annointed our feet and hands and necks.
You gave us love and by and by,
The lessons you gave taught us all how to fly.

I look at myself and feel much richer,
Thanks Sean for giving me the bigger picture.
I am a child of God, filled with love and light,
In the mirror now I am a beautiful sight.
I rise in the morning and have quiet time,
I know this space is Gods and mine.
I feel at peace and go with the flow,
Onwards and upwards, that's where I'll go.

Thank you Sean for sharing your space,
Thank you Sean for love, light and grace.
At Chapel Gap an angel I did see,
He goes around barefoot and tells you "Just be".

Janet Quigley
Student TCCP Therapist October 2004

Acknowledgements

This book would not have been possible had it not been for the love and support that I have received from Rob, my Anam Cara, my family, my clients, our therapists, students therapists and many friends.

However, there are a few who do stand out and I would like to thank my special friends Gordon, Rita and therapists from the Fellowship of Healers, Paul and Pauline, Kath Yates, Glenis, Elsie, Richard, Joan, Steve, Gertie and Eric at Ard Na Ri. Denise, Sharon, Joan our postmistress, the volunteers at our village post office here in beautiful Storth and not forgetting our pooches, Ms Ellie, Lord Winston, Ruby, Poppy, Tilly, Spot, Bobby and Harley.

I should like to thank a special group of colleagues who have become friends and who have made it possible for me to take our beautiful Angel Healing & Retreat Days to **Ireland,** Mairead Conlon, Angela, Bernie Markey and Siobhan Fitzpatrick. **England**: Sue and Krysia of Sheffield Reiki Group; June Eyre, Alison Knox, Margaret Holt, Lesley Turner, Sue Kiley, Sylvia, Lesley, Vivie, and June Watson. **Wales:** Sandra Allen, Nigel and Helen Rushforth. **Scotland**: Aggie, Glen, Joe and the team at the Phoenix Centre in Glasgow. **Madeira**: Gaynor, Graca and Angela.

To Helen at www.search-engine-optimizations.org for the permission to use the web images for the redesign of the book cover. To Tany at Anthony Lowe Publishers and Michelle for their support in bringing the draft to print.

To my clients for their sharing and gifts of love. Some stand out like angel dust and they are, Gail, Sue, Ramo, Hilary and Krysia for their poems, Elsie, Joan and Steve, Brian, Sr Agatha, Sophia Flannery, Jimmy France at Luk Luk Productions, Peter and Rosemary, Elaine and Volunteers at the Gorton Monastery Project, Mary Hindle, Gabrielle and Jeremy Parr for his beautiful music for our recordings and many others who would prefer that I don't mention them by name. Thank you all. Sean.

FORWARD

As we make our way through this brash world, this harsh, noisy, insensitive world, sometimes we come across an oasis of peace and calm that reunites us with our inner purpose and understanding.

It may be a still pool or lake, a clearing in a forest, the middle of a vast meadow or on the banks of a tranquil stream. Contact with the energies and light of the angelic realms through the tireless work of Sean is such an oasis, and rekindles within us a recognition of the knowledge within and a realisation of our place and purpose in the World, and indeed the Universe.

The name of Sean Bradley was on the lips of many of my students and healers before we finally met at a busy, bustling event. The instantly recognisable aura of this dedicated man of peace, love and light preceded him, and once again despite the surrounding clamour, here was that oasis, tempered with the qualities of determination and integrity, the hallmark of a man on a spiritual mission. Since that time the Fellowship have been happy and honoured to support and work alongside Sean. His work with Therapeutic Channelling of the healing energies of the angelic realms in divine partnership with the Christ healing energy is an exciting breakthrough in the healing of the spiritual impoverishment affecting all of God's people on our planet today, bringing light into an otherwise darkened World.

There once was a time when I thought that angels were the stuff of children's stories and prayers or something in biblical texts. Experience has taught me different. I have been blessed to exchange energies with angels, experienced the intensity of their light and the power of their love. They have been seen alongside me in my work by gifted observers and described in detail, and I have observed them through inner sight in their radiance and magnificence. I have experienced an angel gather up a grown woman in great need, enfold her in the wings and nurse her like a baby. There was no need to tell her of this later; she had already confirmed the experience of the healing, comforting love and protection herself. A non-physical friend of mine says, "The only hope for the World today is Love and Truth".

The search for Truth takes many forms and follows many pathways. All are valid as there is no absolute Truth. We must listen to and evaluate all others' truths, then make our own truth. Truth is, as we perceive it to be.

It is through this understanding that The Fellowship of Healers and Sean's Academy are connected through a mutual respect for each other and through networking together we can see a way forward for all who provide any form of healing be it spiritual, energy healing, angelic aesthetic or indeed any other form of bathing humanity in Love.

In our daily lives we focus on the material, physical reality around us yet our true reality is that of the non-physical world of thought and mind. We think they are separate, but they are All One.
Our thoughts are real things with energies of their own. With them we can create. Think Love and create a world of 'Heaven on Earth'.

Love is the healer. Love creates a balance and harmony within our being resonating with higher and deeper Understandings and Realities. Everything we do with Love is a healing, whether it is by aligning with the energies of the angelic realms, by our own intentions to heal ourselves, others, or the planet Earth of which we are part. Simply speak with Love, or with Love in your heart centre be in close proximity to another. We too, all of us, can be an oasis of healing light.

To experience Angelic Love is beyond description. Let us, as a child of our God and a child of His Universe, and in our own way, feel Love passionately within our Being, as an emotion, as energy, as an integral part of Us. With Love we can do anything we want.

Think Love. Every Day.

Gordon L Bagshaw, President of The Fellowship of Healers.

The Author

Sean Bradley, a nurse for 38 years, now gives his time to running courses for clients and practitioners also interested in angelic healing. A former nursing monk is helping people experience the healing touch of angels. Age sixteen, I entered a religious order and trained as a nursing monk. I spent 38 years in nursing, culminating in a mental breakdown aggravated by the adverse side effects of Prozac. My journey has since led me to pastoral counselling and a ministry of spiritual healing, empowering clients and student therapists to reconnect with their 'Inner Child' through their heart centre, embracing the sacred healing energies of the angelic realms and the Divine God/dess within.

Sean, who is based in the Lake District, finds his work brings him clients, in particular, Reiki Masters and Therapists from around the world. He has developed a unique course that empowers clients, therapists and students who are interested in discovering how the Christ and the Four Spheres of Angels can help heal the inner-child and re-learn how to love themselves again, using Therapeutic Channelling, Therapeutic Touch with Sacred Oils.

Born in Glasgow, Sean was brought up in Dublin. He has felt throughout his life that he was being guided and that his life was mapped out. At the age of 16, he entered a monastic community and became a qualified nursing monk, a job that took him to various parts of the world.

A mental breakdown forced him to give up the job he loved but Sean felt that the angels interceded, pointing him in the direction of creating sacred angel peace gardens. He is now a member of the International Federation of Healers (UK) and a member of the Global Forum of Healers. His fascinating book *Angelic Energies has just been* published in America. Due to high levels of interest in Sean's work from all around the world, he has recorded a series of healing meditations / relaxation exercises to empower clients embrace their God/dess and guardian angels, guides and helpers. An experienced teacher, he also offers workshops aiming to open up the human-angel relationship of each participant through the healing and meditative powers of 'Sacred Therapeutic Touch,' empowering clients to reclaim their inner wounded child within. Sean believes that our inner child is our best teacher.

Therapeutic Channelling is another sacred tool in God's toolbox. Each section has been carefully channelled to unlock the 'mystery' and empower student therapists; therapists rediscover an ancient healing that has stood the test of time immemorial.

BEHOLD

ENFOLD

HOLD

LISTEN

TO THE VOICE OF GOD

SPEAK TO YOUR HEART CENTRE

YOUR TEACHER.

Now I Am Free

Though once broken by abuse,
Torn by its ravages and pain,
I now can, al last, see you before me-
Embracing the child within me,
Restoring it to well-being
And thus beholding you.
Throughout my life's journey
I have run away from you.
Scared, helpless, fearful and alone,
Yet through all of this inner-conflict
You led me to a 'safe place,'
This place – my prison cell
Now radiates and reflects
Your love that transforms
The child within!
Though the past 50 years
Have been rescuing years-
Years dominated by:
" Self Denial –self inflicted pain,
All for selfless gain."
Now I have you….My soul imprisoned
In a place of 'Love and Beauty,'
Beholding only You!
Though I sit here alone in my prison cell,
I am not alone!
Surrounded by a myriad of angels
I now know that I am restored, forgiven,
Alive and truly reborn again!
Scared of finding the me within-
Frightened to behold you in
"My Child Within,"
Now I can embrace you in
"My Child Within."
Lovingly I sing your praise –
Praises from a once bruised,
Rejected and isolated heart;

A heart that you created –
A heart, which you restored –
A heart now filled only with
The desire to Follow You.
You are my 'Alpha and my Omega!'
You are my past, present and future.
You are You, I am me.
Together we embrace the –You in me and me in you.
Together we experience the inner joy of
Being Free.
Sean Bradley
H.M.P Kirkham
November 1998.

Seek you first the Kingdom of God and it's righteousness, and all else will be given unto you.

Section 1:

Connecting with the Christ energies and the philosophy of the Essenes.

- How Sean first got involved with sacred energy
- My daily prayer to the energies.
- Message from Christ the healer to our Therapist's in December 2004
- Prayer to Christ the Healer.
- Christ consciousness and 2012.
- Releasing vows under the Lord Christ.

How Sean first got involved with sacred energy

I first got involved with sacred energy as young as the age of 5 when friends would bring to me there sick animals for 'special prayers'. I have always had an affinity with animals and they with me. I guess this is due to the fact that they give unconditional love. In fact, I have always preferred animals to humans and their way of rewarding me for my love and respect towards the animal kingdom was to send me a special friend whom I called my beloved Shimola.

Shimola came into my life during my period of isolation and mental instability as a result of taking a well-known anti depressant. Whilst going through one of my many psychotic, manic episodes during that bleak period between 1995-1998, I now call these my 'Prozac years', I lived a life as if I had inherited a vast fortune. That fortune came from my uncontrolled use of plastic cards. The net result was spiralling debts to the tune of £22.000.

One good thing came from that period of bizarre behaviour. I purchased 4 Westie puppies in Ireland. I gave two of the pups away to my sisters Eileen and Rosemary and kept Ms Ellie and Shimola, then aged 6 weeks old. When the farmer came to my sister Rosemary's front door, he had several puppies in his van. He said that if he couldn't sell the puppy with the damaged nose, he would have to put her down as she wasn't fit to show. I looked into the eyes of this beautiful animal and knew instinctively in my heart that we both had work to do together. Little did I realise that my beloved friend Shimola was to be a source of great inner strength and healing in my life.

When Shimola died on 30 July 2004, my world came to a halt. I went into a deep mourning as I missed my pal. Shimola was the prayer partner who joined me in my nightly quiet times from 11pm –1am. Shimola gave unstintingly and in her short 8 years she touched many hearts here. Several weeks after her passing, I received a beautiful message that was channelled from Shimola through a dear friend. In that message I sensed that because my work in self healing and moving on with my life's work, Shimola's part was now over. I also was told by another client that when they researched the net, they discovered that the name Shimola was Jewish and that it was the name of a Seraphic Archangel. My heart sang God's praises for the knowing and loving I received from His creation.

My dear friend Hilary channelled Shimola's essence in a beautiful painting last October 2004. I have the painting near my quiet prayer corner and I can sense the healing energies flow direct from Shimola into my heart. How blessed we are to have such loving support from our pets.

My faith journey really began when I entered a monastic nursing community in Cobh, Co. Cork in 1966. Over the past 38 years as a professional nurse I have seen every possible ailment, illness, injury both curable and incurable. In February 1972, I was then a second year student nurse on night duty on a busy medical ward in Manchester. My faith in a loving God was tested. One of my patients, a 24 yr. old man, married with 2 young children and whose wife was 8 months pregnant, asked me " Sean, am I dying?" I made every excuse to run away and hide. I made my excuses and broke down crying in the staff-room. I suddenly realized how hard it was to be a nursing monk, offering no words of practical support. My patient who had become a dear friend was dying of Leukaemia and bleeding to death. I felt inadequate; I was devastated and I knew that I had to respond. All I could do was sit by the bedside of my friend and by taking hold of his hand send love and comfort into his soul / spirit. Yes, I was in pieces and shed many tears that night. I was thrown in at the deep end and had to cope with the painful experience of been caught up in the mystery of pain, death and dying. When I look back on that incident, almost 28 years ago, I can say that my friend's dying left a blessing on my soul. I was privileged to be a part of his final farewell with dignity and peace. I was only 26 myself but the whole experience was to equip me with the necessary skills and hands on experience for when I became a nurse specializing in pain control in a rural community in North Wales in the 90's.

My disability (mental illness) has become the realm's ability to touch lives today and lead many beautiful souls back to their God/dess. I am thankful that the lessons learnt and the lessons taught have inspired me not to wallow in self-pity and negativism, but to walk humbly with my God in trust.

My Daily Prayer to God

Holy Father /Mother God, I ask for the fresh outpouring of the Holy Spirit together with the support from the Lord Jesus, Holy Mother Mary, St Francis, St. Clare, St. Colette, St. Mary Magdalene, St Padre Pio; The Archangels Michael, Gabriel, Zadkiel, Raphael, Uriel and Metatron and all the Archangels, Healing angels, my Guardian Angel and all guides who work for the divine light, to now assist, cleanse me of all negative impurities and strengthen, both me and my clients in your healing work.

I now invite, invoke and ask that I be blessed by God and prepared as a channel of Divine love for all who now seek healing of mind-body and soul.

I ask that you bless my being –these humble hands and that you accept all that I am in service of these sacred healing energies.

I thank you for accepting me as a child of God.

Christ's Message to us for 2005

I have come to you that you may have spiritual life to the full!

I am one with you!

I am in the air that you breathe right now!

BEHOLD - Enfold - HOLD - LISTEN

21st December 2012 is a significant date for all Light Workers. On that date the healing energies of the new Adam (Christ) and Eve (Mary Magdalene) will become apparent to you.

Rejoice -Celebrate -get ready for we have now entered a new phase of Christ Consciousness.

Show Love and Compassion to ALL!

In every situation give thanks!

Prayer to Christ the Healer

In the comfort of your love,
I pour out to you my Lord Christ,
The memories that haunt me,
The anxieties that perplex me,
The fears that stifle me,
The sickness that prevails upon me,
And the frustration of all the pain that
Weaves about within me.

Lord Christ help me to see
Your peace in my turmoil,
Your compassion in my sorrow,
Your forgiveness in my weakness,
And your love in my need.

Touch me O Lord Jesus Christ, with your healing power, and strength
That I may be empowered to connect with my inner wounded child.

I call upon you Lord Christ that you will flood my mind-my body and my spirit with the pure healing selfless love of the Creator Spirit.

Open the eyes of my spirit to see my inner beauty and reclaim that childlike innocence so that I can see –reclaim - touch –heal and restore my inner wounded child releasing it to you and the Light of God.

Empower me to reach that part of my being that needs to hear your message of selfless love.
Empower me now to heal myself by taking back my Power and control.
Infuse within my being with the angelic energies that will support me in my faith journey.

As your child, I send you my love and gratitude for walking with me every step of my life.

June 21st 2004

BEHOLD – HOLD – ENFOLD – LISTEN

To the beating heart of Christ Consciousness

Prepare you for 21.12.2012

God's Everlasting Comfort

When life becomes challenging, do you ever just want to run away from it?

To a place where no one knows you, and your problems are all erased?

You just want to find a hole, crawl into it, and hide….maybe forever?

Do you wish you were a child; again, depending upon someone else to take care of whatever life's challenges may come?

Just to be held and told that everything is all right, and there is no need to worry?

In our Bible, Deuteronomy Ch: 33 vs: 27 state, "The eternal God is thy refuge, and underneath are the everlasting arms."

Whenever the challenges of life seem to be too much to handle – whenever you wonder what God was thinking when he laid a particular burden upon you, because surely you are not strong enough to bear it- God is there for you

God is there to hold you, in spirit. God guides you towards all solutions, all answers. God guides to you, all people, all resources, all sustenance that you need, each and every day.

We imagine, in our minds, that we let go, mentally, emotionally, and physically, all that worries us, all that causes us anxiety, and all that causes us fear.

As we imagine letting go, we can imagine God's everlasting arms holding us. Holding us closely and safely.

As we imagine being held by God, our breathing becomes easy and gentle. Our minds become calm and peaceful. Our bodies relax. Our emotions settle into Divine tranquillity.

As we rest, we are renewed by God's strength surging through us.

God's strength, God's intelligence, God's imagination are all ours to use within our lives. As we let go, we let God work and play through us, bringing us through our challenges. Bringing us to God's absolute peace.

Throughout the day, we are reminded that God is with us, guiding us through each and every decision. We can depend upon God to guide us, effortlessly, safely, and loving. God tells us that everything is all right; there is no need to worry.

Prayer of St Francis

Lord make me a channel of your peace,
That where there is hatred, I may bring love,
That where there is wrong,
I may bring your spirit of forgiveness and love.
That where there is discord, I may bring harmony.
That where there is error, I may bring truth.
That where there is doubt, I may bring faith.
That where there is despair, I may bring hope.
That where there are shadows, I may bring Thy Light.
That where there is sadness, I may bring joy.
Lord, grant that I may seek rather
To comfort than be comforted;
To understand that to be understood;
To love than to be loved;
For it is in giving that one receives;
It is by self-forgetting, that one finds.
It is by forgiving that one is forgiven;
It is by dying – that one awakens to eternal life.
The animals of the Earth are among God's very special creatures; they help us work, carry us, guard our homes at night, and best of all, they bring us joy and laughter.
St Francis of Assisi

WE HOLD THIS TRUTH

That all human beings are
created different. That
every human being has
the right to be mentally
free and independent.
That every human being
has the right to feel, see,
hear, sense, imagine,
believe or experience
anything at all, in any
way, at any time.
That every human being
Has the right to behave in
Any way that does not
harm others or break fair
and just laws.
That no human being shall
Be subjected without
Consent to incarceration,
Restraint, punishment, or
Psychological or medical
Intervention in an attempt
To control, repress, or alter
the individual's thoughts,
feelings or experiences.
(Universal declaration of mental rights and freedoms)

The Law of Attraction.

The Law of Attraction states that whatever you focus upon, you attract and manifest into your life to support you, your business and clients.

Advertising your business using the L.O.A. promote your business through affirmations, visualizations and prayer each day.

Simple Prayer:

I ask that everyone who'd receive blessings from my workshops, website and materials be guided to attend further courses, Retreats, or 1 to 1 treatments /counselling sessions. I ask that those lightworkers, carers and others who are searching for information about my work, receive that information. I ask that they be given enough money, time, babysitting, transportation, and all other support, so that they may attend to the workshop. I trust that all prayers are answered.

Worrying about marketing your project simply lowers the energy of the entire project, and that will only attract problems, headaches and people who won't appreciate or 'get' your product. Better to approach any project with love and faith, to attract wonderful support and circumstances. I can't tell you how many miracles I've experienced, where lovely and wonderful people have offered to help me from out of the blue because they were attracted to the energy of my workshops and products.

Don't worry about HOW you'll be helped. The HOW is up to the divinely creative universal wisdom of Light and Love. Instead, focus upon seeing; feeling, and affirming that love surrounds and supports you and your project…..and release it to the universe with full faith.

Those who do attract audiences and publishers are the Lightworkers who are:

a. Teaching about topics, which mirror their personal passions and interests. This is different from lecturing or writing on a topic because it is marketable, or because another speaker or author is having worldly success with the topic. You've got to teach and write about topics, which you are enthusiastic about, or you won't be operating from the Law of Attraction.

b. Those who surround and support their projects with prayer, visualization, and affirmations. These are the Lightworkers who are operating out of faith and they're attracting audiences and publishers! They're open to receiving Divine guidance about their projects, and this guidance truly does steer us in fruitful directions.

The bottom line is that love is the highest vibrational energy, which creates and manifests the results, which are truly joyful for everyone involved.

Ask the Archangel Michael to remind you and teach you about your life's purpose, and to guide your steps in creating a service based project, which will bring great blessings to the world. Not only will you enjoy the benefits, but so will all of the beings whose lives you touch. Blessings to you, lightworker, for your service of light and love.

Angel tips:

Whenever you're around someone who's experiencing stress, guilt, anger, or sadness, your body becomes confused and thinks that these emotions belong to you.

That's why you feel residual emotions after being around the emotional person. The Angels advise us to have a conversation with our body. The body is an elemental type of spirit energy and it needs to be consulted and consoled.

Tell your body, "These emotions belong to (name of person). They don't belong to me or to you." Your body will then release the other person's energies, and you'll feel lighter and freer.

Hate is not overcome by hate
Hate is overcome by Divine Love
Dhampada

Section 2:

Christ and the Philosophies of the Essenes.

- **Christ and the Essenes.**
- **A Poem to Mary Magdalene and Christ**
- **The Philosophy of the Essenes connecting with the Father through angelic energy**
- **The Benedictus and Magnificate.**

of Therapeutic Channelling using the Christ /Angelic ; energies, underpinned by the philosophies of the Essenes.

Therapeutic Channelling has its roots in the ancient teachings of the Essenes dating back to 3000 years BC and the first century of the Christian era at the Dead Sea in Palestine and at Lake Mareotis in Egypt. In Palestine and Syria the members of the brotherhood were known as Essenes and in Egypt as Therapeutae, or healers. They sent out healers, teachers and therapists from the brotherhoods, amongst them were Elijah, John the Baptist, John the Beloved and the great Essene Master, Jesus.

The origin of the brotherhood is said to be unknown, and the derivation of the name is uncertain. Some believes it comes from Enoch, and claim him to be there founder, their Communion with the angelic world having first been given to him.

Records of the Essene way of life have come down to us from writings of their contemporaries. Many spoke of them variously as " a race by themselves, more remarkable than any other in the world," "the oldest of the initiates, receiving their teaching from Central Asia," "teaching perpetuated through an immense space of ages," "constant and unalterable holiness." Echoes of the teachings exist today in many forms, in rituals and in the seven-branched candlestick, in the greeting "Peace be with you," used from the time of Moses.

From its antiquity, its persistence through the ages, it is evident the teaching could not have been the concept of any individual or any people, but in its interpretation, by a succession of great Teachers, of the Law of the universe, the basic Law, eternal and unchanging as the stars in their courses, the same now as two or ten thousand years ago, and as applicable today as then.

The teaching explains the Law, shows how man's deviations from it are the cause of all his troubles, and gives the method by which he can find his way out of his dilemma.

To the earlier concepts of the tree the Essenes added what the ancient writers called Angelology. This Science of the Angels was brought forth by the Essenes at their brotherhood in Palestine. Their angels were the forces of the universe. It was known by many of the ancient peoples that these invisible forces were a source of energy and power, and that man's life was sustained by contact with them. They knew that to the degree man was able to utilize these forces, he would move forward in his individual evolution in body and spirit, and as he put himself in harmony with them, his life would prosper. Certain of the people not only knew of these forces but had specific methods of contacting and utilizing them.

The use of the number seven is an integral part of the Essene tradition – take for example the seven days of the week.

Contact with the angelic forces represented by the Tree of Life was the very essence of the daily life of the Essenes. They knew that to be in harmony with these forces they must make conscious effort to contact them. Furthermore, they considered that to put himself into harmony with the forces of the Heavenly Father and the Earthly Mother was man's most important activity in life.

They also understood the relationship between the forces. They considered that each heavenly force has an earthly force corresponding to it and each earthly force a corresponding heavenly power. The forces which corresponds with each other, above and below, are as follows:

The heavenly Father and the Earthly Mother
The Angel of Eternal Life and the Angel of Earth
The Angel of Creative Work and the Angel of Life
The Angel of Peace and the Angel of Joy
The Angel of Power and the Angel of the Sun
The Angel of Love and the Angel of Water
The Angel of Wisdom and the Angel of Air.

Thou hast made known unto me
Thy deep, mysterious things.
All things exist by Thee
And there is none beside Thee.
By Thy Law
Thou hast directed my heart
That I set my steps straight forward
Upon right paths
And walk where Thy presence is.
From the Book of Hymns V11 of the Dead Sea Scrolls

The Law was planted to reward the children of Light
With healing and abundant peace,
With long life,
With fruitful seed of everlasting blessings,
With eternal joy
In immortality of eternal Light.
From "The Manual of Discipline" of the Dead Sea scrolls.

I am grateful, Heavenly Father,
For thou hast raised me to an eternal height
And I walk in the wonders of the plain.
Thou gavest me guidance to reach Thine eternal company
From the depths of the earth.
Thou hast purified my body
To join the army of angels of the earth
And my spirit to reach
The congregation of the heavenly angels.
Thou gavest man eternity
To praise at dawn and dusk
Thy words and wonders
In joyful song.

From the "Thanksgiving Psalms" of the Dead Sea scrolls V1(iii, 19.36)

FOR CHRIST AND MARY

The face of Christ his beauty shows,
Like the radiance of a new bloom rose.
His life was given to save us all,
And upon our knees we all should fall.

To give thanks to this man,
the Son of God,
Who gave us freedom
for the paths we have trod.
In peace and harmony,
in love and bliss,
His very feet, Mary Magdalene would kiss.

The strength of their bond,
should show us all,
The strength of Love throughout a "fall".
The pain of what they must have borne
Would tear through a heart,
leaving it tattered and torn.

But…in death there is life,
where again we will meet.
To honour our Lord and kneel at His feet.
Hilary Morgan 2004

Embracing Christ Consciousness through the Heart Chakra.

Centuries ago, the ancients living in the Middle East were given a set of divine rules that would help them to walk the path of faith and experience the bountiful blessing from their God. The prophet Moses was inspired to leave the crowd and seek solace high up the mountain of God. Moses knew in his heart that God had a special purpose for him and in his willingness to accept the prompting of Spirit; he embarked on a sacred journey that would change the course of his life and the lives of God's chosen people. Moses accepted from God 10 specific commandments that would safeguard them in their faith journey towards the light.

Today, you and I are personally invited to embrace the divine essence of God in Jesus Christ. Jesus invites us to embrace the Christ consciousness in love. If we are willing to walk this spiritual path with Jesus Christ then we believe and accept that it will lead us to our God /dess. In our acceptance we embrace the Christ consciousness as a new way of life. Living in the Christ Consciousness we are invited to adopt specific core values that will empower us to self heal and reclaim our dignity as sons and daughters of God. They are identical to the 10 commandments that God Yahweh gave to Moses in the desert thousands of years ago. The only difference is that two commandments or core values stand out –they are Love and Light. Love represents loving God in yourself; your neighbour and everything or anything that lives, moves and has their being from God. The Light represents the presence of the divine in all – in you and me –the landscapes –the elements – the animal kingdom – the seasons. Love and Light unites the God in us –in you and in me. Love and Light is Christ Consciousness. When we say to our friends or sign our correspondence with Love and Light we are in fact making a positive statement. We are saying that Christ consciousness is alive -well and kicking! When we embrace Love and Light we are showering divine blessedness throughout the universe. Connecting with our heart centre is essential as it releases the important spiritual triggers that infuse us with clarity of perception and integrity of spirit.

When we embrace the divine love and light of Christ consciousness we are empowered to connect with our own inner child through our heart centre. If we discover that in our woundedness we are trapped then we can release everything to the divine light of God. Pain stored within our emotional blocks and memories is the fuel that propels us to towards our ascension. When we transmute through our high heart chakra, all negative energies associated with deep-rooted pain, shame, unforgiveness, resentment, harboured grudges, lack of self-respect we become infused with Love and Compassion. These two virtues empower us to seek wholeness through our daily aspirations and efforts that will eventually remove all the layers that have held us back in our walk towards ascension.

Our ascension is a step-by-step process of –releasing, clearing and cleansing our emotional blockages layer by layer. As each layer is removed, we attain a higher level of understanding of the divine mystery of Christ consciousness and our individual DNA is recoded empowering us to transcend to a higher vibrational energy. Love and compassion are the keys that facilitate this process and the more we let go and permit God to be in our Minds-in our bodies and in our dealings with self –with others, our higher self accelerates and ascends.

When we connect with our heart centre we touch the very fibres of our being. As a child of the light – a child of God, we embrace the Divine within us. Our heart centre is the consciousness of Christ in God. The Christ consciousness empowers us to look at yourself through the eyes of unconditional selfless healing love. When we engage with our own divinity there is an immediate raising of our spiritual awareness that we are one with God and God is one with us.

We are taken to a place where only divine love reigns supreme – immediately, we are made aware that as a child of God, basking in the Divine rays of the Christ consciousness, that we are perfect, whole, complete. There is no room for negative thought patterns. The love that we experience is of a high vibrational energy and the healing rays emanating from the heart of Christ Consciousness inspires us to reclaim our individuality – our divine gifting as sons and daughters of God – brothers and sisters of Christ.

In the presence of this absolute, unconditional healing love and light of Christ we are empowered to take back our control and personal power. If we are willing to accept this personal invitation our own deep rooted pain and hurts are transmuted into Love and compassion.

According to John O Donohue, he says that "normally the priority in our culture is to function and do what is expected of us. So many people feel a deep dissatisfaction and an acute longing for a more real life, a life that allows their souls to come to expression and to awaken; a life where they could discover a different resonance, one which echoes their heartfelt dreams and deep spiritual longing. No one wants to remain a prisoner in an unlived life. This was the intention of Jesus: ' I have come that you may have life and have it to the full'. Of the many callings in the world, the invitation to the adventure of the awakened and full life of ascension is the most exhilarating. This is the dream of every heart. Yet most of us are lost or caught in forms of life that exile us from the life we dream of. Most people long to step onto the path of creative change that would awaken their lives to beauty and passion, deepen their contentment and allow their lives to make a difference".

That path has indeed arrived and you and I are invited by Jesus Christ to join him and experience pure, selfless unconditional healing love. Jesus is Cohan of the 6th Ray, which is indigo –the ray of devotion –religion and idealism.

Christ consciousness has been around for a long time. It is a flowing energy that is seen as light energy. This energy stimulates our DNA to progress to a deeper level of spirituality. The Christ Consciousness is a level of awareness where you know longer see error in any action that you do or in any other human being – but see only the beauty and perfection in all things. Christ consciousness does not judge as it seeks wisdom, Divine truth, true happiness and total perfection. The concept of Christ consciousness is truly an exquisite one. In essence it means to see the world through the heart / mind of God. The sole purpose of this incarnation is to glorify the Christ consciousness on the earth – in the lives with whom you come in contact, and to live the same thyself. The key to building up your Christ consciousness is to deny all negative ego thoughts from entering your conscious mind from self or others and to keep your mind thinking, affirming and visualizing only Christ thoughts –Xt images at all times. It only takes 21 days to cement a habit into the subconscious mind, so the more you practice this, the more habitual, in a positive sense, it will become.

If you truly want to operate out of Christ consciousness, which I hope you do, as it is one of the primary keys to integrated ascension, you certainly can! To achieve this, however, your utmost attention is demanded in any and every situation along with absolute honesty and integrity.

There is no shame in observing where your weaknesses are. In fact, just the opposite is true. The divine light of Christ that reveals the muddiest waters within self- is the same Christ light that cleanses and purifies them. Courage to face self and a willingness to change join with our lesser attributes when we offer them up at God's sacred alter. When this is done, then that which is a block from Christ consciousness, namely fear in its many guises and judgement in its many forms, will be transcended and transmuted into divine love and light.

Christ consciousness is a way to manifest God upon the Earth. It is life at its most glorious capacity, a place of pure connection with our brothers and sisters, with self and GOD. When we achieve our own ascension or the seven levels of initiation, now considered to be Master level, one should not become complacent. As a Master we cannot let down our vigilance. I believe that the old biblical statement still holds true "After Pride cometh the fall". One has to work with the same self-discipline and single focus and commitment after ascension as one did before.

Embracing this new way of life invariably causes us to loose friends – friends who wish to stay in victim hood. Living in Christ consciousness, empowers us to abandon any connection with victim – or with anyone living victim hood, or who are asleep in 3D.

Embracing the Christ consciousness is a way of life that lives forever. It has no end that we know of. When we are living in the oneness of Jesus in the Christ Consciousness we are living out of the essence of love, compassion, respect, reverence and devotion to the cause of spiritual reawakening preparing many for the 21 December 2012. This is a significant day for all light workers who in their physical ascension will move from 3 dimensional energy to 5th dimensional energy.

The year 2008 is another significant year for the universe. I believe that the Crystal Children will have come of age and will come together from the 4 corners of the globe to facilitate a major shift in universal consciousness in how we are living life right now. Wolf Moondance once said, where in history has mankind taken such a brutal turn to do the things that we do to the planet – the animal kingdom and to each other.

I am of the opinion that we live in end times and that the time is now upon us when we will have to make positive choices in order to safeguard this beautiful planet of ours. The Crystal Children will come of age in 2008. Some of you may have already recognised them gathering discreetly in readiness for 2008. By that time, they will be in their late teens, early 20's making a profound impact upon the entire world. They will with one voice condemn the greed, violence and inhumanity of man to man. The army of Crystal Children will rally round to support all light workers who have become 'battle weary'. They will be the beating heart of selfless love in action. They will become that mighty spiritual army of Christ consciousness on Earth. They will set the scene and prepare the world for 2012.

21.12 2012 is the Dawn of the new Aquarius. According to many angelologists, it represents Christ's second coming. I don't see Christ's second coming with fire and brimstone as predicted by the prophets. I see a new dawn – the beginning of the end of the old ways of thinking and the dawn of a new beginning. Something wonderful will happen on 21. 12.2012. my life will change for the best. I am totally committed to living my life now in the Christ Consciousness and my commitment is renewed each and every day.

The work that I do is to hopefully re-awaken the dormant spirit that exists in mankind. Working in partnership with the angelic energies empowers me to Channel the Christ healing energies through therapeutic touch thereby resurrecting the Christ consciousness within us all.

In my late night, early morning quiet times between 11pm and 1am each night, I join up with our therapists and my friends who are the Poor Clare Collettine enclosed nuns around the world in silent devotional prayer.

I believe that silence is the sister of the divine and in that silence we are aware of a loving presence of selfless unconditional love touching and restoring our heart centre to listen attentively to the voice of Christ and of God. The Angelic and Christ energies have assured me that on 21.12.2012 there will be a revelation that will create a stir for all mankind. Christ will return along with his beloved disciple, Mary Magdalene. They will appear as the new Adam and Eve and they will be perceived and recognised not by their physical attributes but by the vibrational healing energy rays that will flow from them through us to each other and us. We will be transformed from 3rd Dimension to 5th Dimensional energy. Those who wish to remain locked in 3D will be taken to another place where they will have to relive their life experience and learn their life lessons all over again.

We who have willingly embraced the Christ Consciousness will automatically be transformed and renewed into the Christ consciousness and in the words of St Francis. We will Behold – Hold - Enfold –and Listen to the beating heart of God through Christ consciousness. Our 3D lives will have ceased on 21.12.2012 and we will have entered 5D for infinity. We will have learned our life lesson and be escorted back home to Paradise where we will Behold the presence of God –where we will be enfolded by Divine beauty forever. Where we will hold firm to the truth that we are co heirs with Christ and in our hearts we will listen to the sacred voice of spirit sing God's divine praises to us.

Our journey in Christ consciousness will carry on as we ascent nearer to the throne of selfless love and light.

Know that I am with YOU always, even to the 'end of day'.

Jesus

The Essenes's prayer said by Mary

Within the Most High, my soul blossoms,
Leaps for joy at the sight of the ascendant path.
What is on high came to meet what is below,
And the Most High has impregnated my soul through his radiant look.
Out of all the generations, mine is blissful,
For the Almighty did great things for me;
He impregnated my soul.
Holy is his name; through the centuries runs his blessing
For those who, because of love, remain faithful to Him.
Sublime and untouched is the Most High,
Almighty is the power of his arm;
He scatters the proud, destroys those who only think of themselves,
Turns down the throne of those who only believe in their own power,
And lifts the humble, the simple, the pure and loving hearts up to his kingdom.
He showers with his gifts those who remain silent before Him.
The Most High never gives up his children who serve him with wisdom and love, amen. (Gospel according to St. Luke 1. vs: 46-55).

REFLECTION FOR YOUR TIME IN SILENCE

Please use this time of silent reflection to enjoy stillness and as you breathe in the breath of Divine Love into your heart centre (your higher self) Behold –Enfold –Hold- Listen to the voice of the Archangel Gabriel, God's Messenger, speak to YOU.

- **"He impregnated my soul" –what is this statement saying to your heart right now?**
- **" He showers with his gifts those who remain silent before Him"- what is this saying to you?**
- **"The Most High never gives up on His children;" what are these words saying to you today"?**

In your quiet times before Source whilst in the presence of the angelic realms, light your candle and sense now the presence of the Archangel Gabriel speak to your heart centre and affirm you as a Child of God. You are whole, perfect and complete as a light worker, working for the Light of selfless love in a modern chaotic world that needs your light.

In the final meditation when the Archangel Gabriel comes before you and says "***Hail full of Grace, God is with you, Blessed art thou amongst women, and blessed is the fruit of thy womb,"*** impregnating your mind-body and spirit' with the precious love and Light of God – Christ Consciousness. Will you be like Zechariah and disbelieve or be like Mary and Elizabeth and ACCEPT the promise " **For there is nothing that God cannot do for YOU today**."

Will your reply be: "**may it happen to me as you have said**."

THE ESSENES

The Essenes themselves, lived apart from the rest of the community at large, preferring to live as a Brotherhood, during the last 2 or 3 centuries B.C. and the first century of the Christian era. They were found by the shores of the Dead Sea, and on the shores of Lake Mareotis in Egypt, where they were known as Therapeutae.

(The Teachings of the Essenes from Enoch to the Dead Sea Scrolls E.B. Szekely p.11)

Traces of the fundamental principals were taught in ancient Persia, Egypt, India Tibet, China, Palestine, Greece and many other countries- this, probably due not only to the validity of their Divine origins, but also to the fact that they do have the potential to solve the World's problems.

The Essenes knew that there were tens of thousands of Angels, each with their individual tasks to fulfill, there being 4 CHOIRS of angels, these are described as:

1st Choir-COUNSELLORS- Seraphim, Cherubim, Throes
2nd Choir-GOVERNERS- Dominions, Virtues, Powers
3rd Choir- MESSENGERS- Principalities, Archangels, Angels
4th Choir-NATURE WAVE- concerned with 4 universal Life -Force elements Earth, Fire Water and Air realms.

They worked with the angels of air, earth, fire and water (among others), AS DID JESUS- when He walked on water, calmed the storm, and performed other such miracles. It is believed that Jesus learned how to do this when He lived with the Essenes.

They also knew that the mind consists of both a conscious and sub-conscious section, and that these can be re-programmed to be more positive, by using positive affirmations, the first thing at morning, noon and last thing at night. In this respect and others, they were considered to be the ' Fathers 'of Psychology.

The Essenic beliefs appear to epitomize the common denominator of all religions, as these have influenced other major world religions such as: Brahmanism, the Vedas, the Upanishads, the Yoga systems of India, as well as Judeo/ Christian religions -

Who all accept the existence of angels? Indeed, the word Angel- is believed to derive from the Greek word- 'Angelos', meaning,'messenger'.

The teachings have also contributed much to western culture, Freemasonry, Gnosticism, the Kabala and Buddha's Bodhi Tree - correlates with the Essenic Tree of Life.

COMMUNING WITH THE ANGELIC REALM IS **CENTRAL TO ESSENIC TEACHINGS, AS IT IS TO THERAPEUTIC CHANNELLING.**

PROLOGUE TO THE COMMUNIONS

"I ENTER THE ETERNAL AND INFINITE GARDEN, WITH REVERENCE TO THE HEAVENLY FATHER, THE EARTHLY MOTHER AND GREAT MASTERS, REVERENCE TO THE HOLY, PURE AND SAVING TEACHING, REVERENCE TO THE BROTHERHOOD OF THE ELECT."

THE ESSENE COMMUNIONS ARE AS FOLLOWS:

MONDAY MORNING - Angel of Life
"ANGEL OF LIFE, ENTER MY LIMBS _ AND GIVE STRENGTH TO MY WHOLE BODY".

He / she contemplates trees as he feels himself absorbing vital forces from trees and forests.

MONDAY EVENING- Angel of Peace

"PEACE, PEACE, PEACE ANGEL OF PEACE, BE ALWAYS EVERYWHERE.

He contemplates the moon and the moonlight invoking and visualizing universal peace in all spheres of existence.

TUESDAY MORNING- Angel of Joy
"ANGEL OF JOY, DESCEND UPON EARTH, AND GIVE BEAUTY TO ALL BEINGS."

He feels himself absorbing feelings of joy from the beauties of nature as he contemplates the colures of sunrise of sunset, the song of a bird the aroma of a flower

<u>TUESDAY EVENING</u>- Angel of Power

"ANGEL OF POWER, DESCEND UPON MY ACTING BODY AND DIRECT ALL MY ACTS."

He feels the cosmos-vital forces from the stars being absorbed by the nervous system of the acting body, as he contemplates the stars, their radiations and the cosmic ocean of life.

<u>WEDNESDAY MORNING</u>- Angel of the Sun

"ANGEL OF SUN, ENTER MY SOLAR CENTRE AND GIVE THE FIRE OF LIFE TO MY WHOLE BODY."

He contemplates the rising sun and feels and directs the accumulated solar forces radiating through his solar plexus, sending them to all parts of his body.

<u>WEDNESDAY EVENING</u>- Angel of Love

"ANGEL OF LOVE DESCENDS UPON MY FEELING BODY AND PURIFY ALL MY FEELINGS".

The Feeling Body both sends and attracts superior currents of feeling to and from all beings on earth and all those in the cosmic ocean of Love.

<u>THURSDAY MORNING</u> -Angel of Water

"ANGEL OF WATER, ENTER MY BLOOD AND GIVE THE WATER OF LIFE TO MY WHOLE BODY."

He contemplates the waters of the earth in rain, river, lake, sea, or anywhere, and the currents of the Angel of Water are felt intensifying and directing the circulation of blood.

<u>THURSDAY EVENING</u>- Angel of Wisdom

"ANGEL OF WISDOM, DESCEND UPON MY THINKING BODY

AND ENLIGHTEN ALL MY THOUGHTS."

Superior thoughts are then sent and attracted by the Thinking Body while the individual contemplates all thought on earth and in the cosmic ocean of thought.

FRIDAY MORNING - Angel of Air
"ANGEL OF AIR, ENTER MY LUNGS AND GIVE THE AIR OF LIFE TO MY WHOLE BODY."

He contemplates the atmosphere and breathes rhythmically.

FRIDAY EVENING -The Heavenly Father
"THE HEAVENLY FATHER AND I ARE ONE."

In time this brings union with the eternal and boundless cosmic ocean of all Superior radiations from all planets, as cosmic consciousness are awakened and the individual is finally united with the Supreme Power.

SATURDAY MORNING- The Earthly Mother
"THE EARTHLY MOTHER AND I ARE ONE.
SHE GIVES THE FOOD OF LIFE TO MY WHOLE BODY."

He contemplates edible fruit, grains or plants and feels the currents of the Earthly Mother flowing in him and intensifying and directing the metabolism of his body.

SATURDAY EVENING- Angel of Eternal Life
"ANGEL OF ETERNAL LIFE, DESCEND UPON ME AND GIVE ETERNAL LIFE TO MY SPIRIT."

He contemplates union with the currents of thought of the superior planets and gains power to overcome the sphere of gravitation of earthly currents of thought.

SUNDAY MORNING- Angel of Earth
"ANGEL OF EARTH, ENTER MY GENERATIVE ORGANS AND

REGENERATE MY WHOLE BODY."

He contemplates the life-generating soil and the growing grass, feeling the currents of the Angel of Earth transforming the reproductive energy into regenerative forces.

<u>SUNDAY EVENING-</u> Angel of Creative Work
"ANGEL OF CREATIVE WORK, DESCEND UPON HUMANITY AND GIVE ABUNDANCE TO ALL MEN."

The contemplation is upon bees at work, and the creative work of humanity all spheres of existence is concentrated upon.

The Essenes also communed with the angels at noon.

The Angels helped the Essenes in every facet of theirs eveyday lives, and the communions were used to ensure that they lived as long and healthy lives as possible - for which they were renowned!

Do you sense that you too were an Essene with Jesus by the Dead Sea?

The Benedictus.

Blessed be the Lord, the God of our ancestors,
He has visited his people and redeemed them.
He has raised up for us a mighty savour
In the house of our ancestors
As he promised by the lips of holy men,
Those who were his prophets from of old.
A savour who would free us from our foes,
From the hands of all those who hate us.
So his love for our fathers is now fulfilled
And his holy covenant remembered.
Our God swore to Abraham our Father to grant us,
That free from fear, and saved from the hands of our foes,
We might serve our God in holiness and justice
All the days of our life in God's presence.
As for you, little child,
You shall be called a prophet of God, the most High,
You shall go ahead of the Lord God
To prepare God's ways before him,
To make known to his people their salvation
Through forgiveness of all their sins,
The loving-kindness of the heart of our God,
Who visits us like the dawn from on high.
Our God will give light to those who are in darkness,
Those who dwell in the shadow of death,
And guide us into ways of peace.
Glory be to the Father of every living Being
That was -That is and that will ever live..
To the Son of God Jesus the holy one;
And to the Spirit of our God who touches everything that lives
–that moves and has their being before God.
To the divine beings who are appointed to watch over us here on Earth.
(Said in the morning by our therapists)

The Magnificat

My soul glorifies the Lord God,
My spirit rejoices in God, my Savour.
He looks on his servant in her lowliness;
Henceforth all ages will call me blessed.

The Almighty works marvels for me,
Holy is His name.
His mercy is from age to age,
On those who fear Him.
He puts forth his arm in strength
And scatters the proud-hearted.

He casts the mighty from their thrones
And raises the lowly.
He fills the starving with good things,
Sends the rich away empty.

He protects those of us, who are servants to the Most High God,
Remembering his mercy.

The mercy promised to our fathers of old,
Abraham and all of his sons and daughters forever.
(Said in the evening by our therapists)

I have called YOU by your name –YOU are mine
Jesus

NOTES:

Section 3:

Connecting with Angelic healing energy

- Message to our Therapists from the Archangel Princes of the Healing Bagua
- Poem " We are touched by Angels"
- Messages from the Archangel Metatron and Source angel to Sean
- Angelic messages from the realms to Sean
- Charkas and Angels.
- Prayer of protection to St Michael.
- The Four Spheres of Angels.
- The Angel Bagua.
- Feedback about the healing Bagua from our Therapists.
- Student feedback to angelic involvement.
- The Onion by Sr Agatha
- Poem by Djwal Khul

Channelled Information from the Christ Energies via the Archangels Metatron, Michael, Gabriel, Raphael, Uriel & Source Angel

The Master said, ***"Whosoever shall not receive the Kingdom of God as a LITTLE CHILD, shall not enter therein."***

This means – that we have to accept the daily experiences and react to them always on a higher level, receiving and giving forth in the Spirit of God, so far as you humanly can, and in accordance with your understanding of God.

These daily and tests of every day, empower you to learn to control the kingdom of yourself. You don't have to be a crank! You are not called to be such a crank!

Be human and express yourself harmoniously. Enjoy life – be God – God, who would have you enjoy the gifts and the fruits of the Earth, and all the beauties of the Earth.

We also have to cultivate that higher self which enables you and I to see the beauty lying behind the physical form of others, of your brother and sister animals, the plants; your companions the glorious mountains (Lungs of the universe) the streams and the wind in the trees; the beauty of the Sun, Moon and the stars of the heavens.

Live harmoniously in this way and you will surely find the God that Jesus told you to love.

The Divas of the angelic realms who control the Powers of Nature would feel utter harmony; respond to the call of a being that had attained perfect mastership.

" The Kingdom of God is within you."

- True religion is not tied to any Creed or Dogma.
- It is not merely some form of belief.
- Religion is the growing consciousness of God in one's own being.
- When a soul becomes awakened to the Light of God, then the Christ within the soul, starts to grow.
- This growing God consciousness is its strength, staying power; its comfort and guide.
- This is True Religion.
- This is what all humanity is searching for.

- People in the West have to a large extent forgone organised religion – but they are still seeking for God in many ways.
- They will not get very far until they learn that the God they seek – Is in themselves.
- We can learn about this vital truth only through the love which they can feel for others and compassion for the sufferings, the harmony and pain which shadow the life of all other human beings.
- Men and women, in their Search for God in Religion, must look beyond the shells of Orthodoxy, Creed, and Dogma, for the indwelling Spirit in all other Beings.
- True Religion in a person gives them complete conviction beyond shadow of doubt, that they cannot die and that those whom they love can never die.

My children – you have been given grave Trust; your responsibility is to make use of the gift of knowledge which has been given to you, because if you do not – if you cover up your Talents of being a Therapeutic Channeller via sacred Touch, and bury it – in future days you may find that you have lost your Talent, which means that in some future life you will have lost your spiritual awareness. Try not to accept such gifts, my children, without due thankfulness. Do not take these gifts for granted.

Realise that the smallest faculty, whatever it maybe, is entrusted to you as a talent to be used for the blessings of others. This also includes the Egg of the Archangel Metatron.

Therefore by constant aspiration make yourself a clear Channel for the pouring through of Divine Light of the Sun; for as Mother Earth receives the sunlight which stimulates and causes the seed to grow, so you, each in your degrees, are that Mother Earth.

When God has given you the Seed, no matter whether it be a seed to plant, or a spiritual seed – which means some attainment of the soul – remember that it is for spiritual sowing. Your spiritual seeds are given to you in Trust, not to keep to yourself, but to sow again in life, so that others may benefit from your sowing and gifting. So it is with Therapeutic Channelling – you were impregnated with the Christ energies and now you are invited to impregnate the universe with these energies through the selfless servant hood of your being in Partnership with the Angelic Realm. You have been invited – called into God's service -you are its true disciples in a world that is spiritually impoverished and in need of the healing love of Christ's healing energies.

The soul can be likened to the Earth, the Mother, and the Sun, the Spirit, the Christ Light, is the seed planted in the heart of every man, woman and child, the Christ Child, that the Earth may be peopled with happiness. God does not condemn human kind to sorrow, to a life of wretchedness.

God has given life to His – Her Sons and Daughters that they may enjoy greater glories. It is therefore our work – your work on Earth, ours in Spirit – to help in the harvesting, the bringing forth of the fruits of the spiritual life upon Earth.

I Am the Bread of Life, said Christ, and the Christ (XT) is within your heart. The Bread of Life reposes in the Sacred Heart Chakra (between the navel and the Heart), but you must endeavour to enter the inner sanctuary and attune yourself to that Power.

You must allow the 'power within you' to come into operation. In this way you are opening yourself to the Divine inflow. Do not be anxious. Just surrender yourself to the all – loving Father –Mother God, for all is love and none of you need fear life –either life here or the life in spirit.

There is nothing to fear at all!

As a Channeller of Christ's healing energies you:

- Were Chosen –Appointed – Anointed to work with the Christ energies as a Co Creator of the Divine Mother God.
- Were touched by Divine Love and empowered to be like Christ in your Servant hood.
- You are now a New Creation – a people (Sisterhood-Brotherhood) set apart to work with God – For God –in and through our God's Love using Christ's healing energies - to reclaim the dignity of your Being and Gifting and Touch Souls for God.

THE WAY FORWARD

To maintain your effectiveness as a Child of God – a Channeller of Divine Healing Love Energies you are now invited to:

- Go forth and set the Minds –Body –Spirit – Souls of our Brothers and Sisters with the Christ Energies and healing love.
- Work in close Partnership with the Archangel Princes of the Healing Trigram and Celestial Bagua using Therapeutic Touch and Channelling of these sacred energies.
- Continue daily contact with your God using the prayers given to you. They are the Benedictus Canticle (Morning Prayer) and the Magnificate (Evening Prayer).
- Quiet times of silence and stillness in your sacred oasis. It is recommended that you initially start with 15 minutes and progress to a level of prayer that suits you and your daily commitments. We recommend that you strive to reach a period of 1 hour daily before your God. The more time you devote to your God in quiet prayer the rewards will be noticed in your daily life and through the positive impact in your clients and gifting as a Therapeutic Channeller.
- We recommend that you maintain effective links with your fellow therapists and meet on a regular basis, i.e. every 4 weeks or monthly.
- Spread the word to clients – colleagues and other Therapists.
- Develop a nurturing Forum that will be self-supporting through the membership's skills and talents.
- Be committed to ongoing training and support. Encourage the members (Sisters & Brothers) to attain their Master's Certificate so as to train others in Therapeutic Channelling in your own locality / country.
- Remember to celebrate your anniversary of qualifying as a Therapeutic Channeller by undertaking a 2-day retreat with your group. Plan this well in advance to avoid disappointment.

You are now ambassadors of the Divine God / dess.

You are committed to working with our God and the entire Angelic Realms by personal invitation only.

Your free will is your gift and your desire is your commitment.
This beautiful land needs to be transformed from organised religion True Religion.

Set my people free as from today!

Be a light shining in the dark and bring the Christ healing –energies and love to as many as you can – Don't Be Afraid – Be Empowered as from NOW!

You are a Child of God – a Child of the Universe –
You are Reclaimed and Renewed.

You are impregnated with Christ's healing energies and selfless love.
You are a Liberated Light Worker.

You have been Chosen and called by name.
Who Am I? I know you by your name…you are forever mine!

I bless you and I Love you.

Thank you for being there for our brothers and sisters in crisis.

Channelled on 17th July 2003
Sean J. Bradley

Touched By Angels

We are touched by Angels
And walk where angels thread,
They will guide us, walk beside us
Through the days ahead.

In the hours of darkness,
When our dreams have flown,
They will bring us hope
And gentle healing,
We are not alone.

In our times of doubting,
Still they understand,
And forever
Touched by angels,
We will walk hand in hand.

(Anon)

Channelled through Arch Angel Metatron

The World was a Gift, from God – From His Heart,
It was given for knowledge, for you All to impart.
It was gifted through Love, and now - to your shame!
You've damaged the Gift, and thrown it back – again!
This time and this chance.
Is the *LAST that HE gives*? In terms of the Earth…
And He will *see how* you live.
You *must* work hard, the repair work to do…
PURE LOVE in energy will bring you all through.
This cleansing and clearing h*ad* to be done
To shock you all into working as one.
The souls who have crossed
Went with *your* bridge of Light, so it just shows you all
What you *can* do in spite of the stupidity and abuse that has been directed into the Gift…You *MUST* pull together now and make the energy LIFT.
It is not too late to turn things around, but better start NOW before Earth is razed to the ground.
This recent "event" has come to show what *can* happen?
As many of you know…when you mess around with balance, when the harmony shifts…
Get started immediately and *use* all of your gifts.
You *must* work together and you ALL now should see
That the *only* "RULER"
Can ever be ME!
You are me in spark, and the light, with which you shine,
Should *show you all*
You only ever *were* MINE.
Too many groups with egos abound…
This one with Reiki that one with sound…
Some say prayer alone s*hould* be the only way

I AM THE *ONE!*
LISTEN TO WHAT *I* SAY!

It is my hand alone that gave you your life…

Time now to learn fast and remove all of this strife.
When *WILL* you learn?
That gentleness and Love from the Heart
Is the greatest of gifts?
That to you all, I did impart?

The Divine

1/2/05

Therapeutic Channelled Messages from the Realms on 12th January 2004.

Therapeutic Channelling is:

- Sacred touch with the Divine One.
- It is a sacred tool connecting God with you and me.
- A sacred tool that connects God with us.
- Empowerment: we are empowered by God to self-heal.
- Released: angelic energies assist us to connect with our inner wounded child and release our pain.
- Reclaimed: the Divine Christ (Xt.) healing energies of the Lord Christ (Ascended Master) with the healing energies of the Archangel princes of the Celestial Bagua empower us to reclaim our dignity and inner beauty.

1. Divine Connection – God to us and we with God (Spirituality)
2. Angelic Connection – Angels with us.
3. Empowerment to self heal all that is broken by man in ignorance and pain.
4. Released: the release of all negative, destructive energies from our being.
5. Reclaimed: we are set free to Live –to Love –to Enfold the presence of the Divine in and around our sacred oasis of Being.

Therapeutic Channelling is a sacred tool given to us by God to use on ourselves to self-heal and others in selfless love.

Through Therapeutic Channelling God connects with His /her people.

Through sacred touch, the angelic energies empower us to self-heal.

Through 'Hope'

MESSAGE FROM THE ARCHANGEL GABRIEL 12.12.04 to Krysia.

Welcome Beloveds to this special day
When great rejoicing comes our way
A mighty feast before us lies
When Heaven once again descends from the skies
To wrap you all in Celestial Love
A gift to God's children from above.
He sends His essence to this world
As His mighty banner is unfurled
To encompass all His children here
To banish want and pain and fear
You are all on a blessed road
To rise above this heavy load
To seek and find the road to home
To know that where e're you roam
You are supported in loving arms
That who you really are cannot come to harm
For the Father / Mother surrounds you with Heavenly Realms
And if you let us we will take the helm
As your ship of life you sail
Seeking your own Holy Grail
So welcome Beloveds, we are close at hand
All around you we stand
So open your hearts that we may enter in
Silence from your minds the din
Set this special day aside
And quietly in our arms abide
And learn the meaning of this season true
And the great blessings it can bring to you
To pass to the others you meet along the way
And we will be ever at your side
As together in our Fathers / Mother's love we all abide.

Angel Poem

Angels coming out to play,
Angels touch our life each day.
Though we may not know they're there,
There are angels everywhere.

Angels can cause a heart to sing.
Angels give our spirits wings!
An angel's touch brings God near.
An angel's smile can dry a tear.

Have you felt a tug on your heartstrings?
Chances are 'twas caused by angel wings.
They flutter softly in the light,
Shimmering with edges of gold so bright.

We mere mortals to earth are bound.
Angels trod on holy ground.
So next time you are feeling low
Remember – angels are there – wherever you go!
anon

Angels Touch Us – Heal Us – Empower Us

Angel Connection Prayer:

Higher Self, lead me to the Vibration level and Light Level of the Angelic-Kingdom.

Angel Mantra:

Eee Nuh Rah Eee Nuh Rah Eee Nuh Rah
Zay Nuh Rah.

(Angels, here I am, I come to be with You).

Named Archangel Princes of the Angel Bagua / Healing Trigram, including their messages.

Archangels welcome diversity and so are champions of our respective individuality, sexuality, ethnicity, religious beliefs / creeds as well as cultural differences.

When we embrace the angelic realms, particularly when we rediscover our angels of the 'Nature Wave,' they transform our oasis or garden into a 'sacred sanctuary' where the Creator lives and where the angels of all Four Spheres dwell. This transformation has a knock-on effect in our lives as well as in our relationships with others. Our spirit is reawakened and our love for God and our angels is no longer dormant but now active and creative. I found it hard at first to connect with the angelic realms because of an innate fear and religious superstition handed down from childhood. However, as with any relationship I had to learn how to love and receive their love. It was like being a child in 'kindergarten, or nursery.' I had to be shown by them how to be still and not be afraid of them. I had to learn the simple basics of how to communicate with angels as well as discerning their messages and respective angelic voices. This did take time but thankfully having sustained a period in the wilderness due to a mental breakdown, I was surprised to discover that 'good always triumphs over every adversity.' I never thought that at the time because I became focussed on my illness and the losses resulting from loosing my job, home and partner of 24 years. Thankfully, I was given the courage to kneel down and humbly ask my guardian angel to help me and the rest is now history! Here I am today sharing with you how to connect, engage and receive angelic guidance and their loving support in your angel peace garden. My knowledge and practical advice is drawn from life's painful experiences.

During that 'dark night of the soul experience,' when I sensed that my life was indeed a failure and that my recent illness coping with severe depression had robbed me unfairly of the ability to nurse and support the sick and dying in my locality I had no alternative but to look upwards instead of feeling so downcast. The future did seem bleak but I sensed that I was being nurtured and supported by the divine and by the presence of angels in and around my garden. I was not a gardener or an expert in angels or even for that matter garden design and horticulture! My tutors were the angels of the Nature Wave and the animal kingdom. What I have learned regarding sacred angel peace gardens was not my doing but theirs. I now sense that throughout my life I have been nurtured to receive the 'Divine Blueprint,' known as the angel Bagua – Healing Trigram and Celestial Placement Square. At first I thought that I had lost the plot and was hallucinating. Never in my wildest dreams did I ever imagine that I would be singled out to be a garden designer who specialised in creating and designing as well as empowering clients through workshops, audio-tapes to experience the presence of their divine Creator God and behold the face of angels in their sacred oasis.

Working with our Archangel Princes in the sacred angel peace garden / oasis has transformed my life as well as enriching my spirituality and understanding of angels and a loving Creator God. Through the simple tasks of pruning, weeding and planting new seedlings for the next season's growth and display I am aware that I am the hands that they use to create and design beauty beyond words. It is the presence and untiring support from the angelic realms that have achieved the Bethany Project here in Manchester. These sacred angel peace gardens have an eclectic feel to them in that they incorporate the sacred influences of major religions and cultures honouring the Creator God within the garden landscapes. I am only the instrument in the Creator's hands. It is the presence of angels that have achieved the ethereal beauty that one experiences when they first enter the gardens here.

But working with our angels here on Earth is important for the total well being of the Earth and its inhabitants. Connecting with these angelic servers is paramount as they are the backroom staff of the sacred oasis. To make that first connection we have to approach the angelic realms with reverence, humility, respect and communicate with' simplicity of heart.' When I first became aware that there are Divas who supervise the trees, plants, flowers, the four elements (air, water, fire, earth) as well as the animal kingdom I was made aware that angels of this realm are hesitant to communicate and work with mankind because of the devastation that man has caused to these kingdoms. I was made aware by the Archangels who supervise these Divas (angels) that I was to stand before them and apologise / repent for man's inhumanity as shown to one's fellow man and the Earth and animal kingdom. Over a period of months, I became aware of their angelic presence and often I would see them working alongside me in the garden. When I go abroad to run workshops I have to inform the Diva angels that I would appreciate their support in the garden. On my return, I am never surprised to see that they have carried on as always!

Connecting with the angels of the Earth realms is not difficult. In fact it is made easy for us with the support of our guardian angels and our Archangels. We don't have to be religious – even a regular churchgoer to access angelic support. What they look for is a sincere, humble, reverent and committed heart that is loving, inviting and all embracing towards the Creator's kingdom.

According to the great St. Thomas Aquinas, " Angels transcend every religion, every philosophy, every creed. In fact, angels have no religion as we know it….their existence precedes every religious system that has ever existed on Earth." Angels represent the Divine and spirituality!

The Creator has entrusted Archangels with unique powers - gifts and specialist skills to place at our disposal that will facilitate our relationships with the Creator. Each area of the Angelic Bagua – Trigram and Celestial Magic Placement Square has already been enriched by the divine universal life force energies for our sole benefit and spiritual, physical and mental well being.

When we are faced with fear, trauma, illness, depression, anxiety, we are advised to stop – stand still- reflect- breathe in the breath of the angelic realms and become totally infused by ethereal – angelic life force energy. Angels are indeed 'Messengers' of the Divine Creator God who though unseen are there all the same working tirelessly behind the scenes, on our behalf. Angels are perceived by some followers as deities in their own right. When we adopt this attitude we do them a great disservice, as they are servants of the divine and not God! They represent the Creator and empower each one of us to make a connection with our spirit and with our personal angel who in turn take us on a personal journey of self-discovery. This faith- spirit journey eventually leads us before the throne of the 'Divine Presence.'

The Angel Bagua – Trigram and Celestial Magic Placement Square are indeed sacred tools that are part of the 'Divine blueprint.' To access their sacred energy, or universal life force angelic energy it is important to know a little about the named Archangel Princes – about who Metatron is and what he does on our behalf. Here we shall take an in-depth look at the named Archangels listed in the Celestial Bagua – Trigram and Celestial Magic Placement Square of the Angel Sacred Peace Garden.

The named Archangel Princes of the Celestial Baqua / Trigram are:

1. **Archangel Michael – Prince of the North.**
2. **Archangel Uriel - Prince of the East.**
3. **Archangel Gabriel – Prince of the South.**
4. **Archangel Raphael – Prince of the West.**
5. **Archangel Metatron – Prince of the Inner Circle of 'Universal Life Force Angelic Energy.'**

The Named Archangels of the Celestial Magic Placement Square are:

1. **Archangel Michael: (North).**
2. **Archangel Melchizedek: (South West).**
3. **Archangel Uriel: (East)**
4. **Archangel Moroni: (South East)**
5. **Archangel Israfael: (Centre of Sacred Oasis).**
6. **Archangel Raziel: (North West).**
7. **Archangel Raphael: (West).**
8. **Archangel Ariel: (North East).**
9. **Archangel Gabriel: (South).**
10. **Archangel Metatron: (Inner Circle).**

1. **Archangel Michael.**

Michael to all intentional purposes appears to be the most well known and seems to be the 'favourite' of all the angels. The name Michael means, "Who is like God" and his is known by other different names and titles given to him by God because of his unquestionable loyalty and devotion to God. Names such as 'Warrior Angel – Angel of Patience – Prince of the Chaldeans." Despite the many titles given to this high ranking angel, Michael will always be there for us as a powerful spiritual ambassador to help us throughout our faith's journey. Michael is depicted as a 'warrior angel' with sword in hand to fight evil. He represents the marginalized as well as the oppressed in our society. Sacred Scholars have led us to believe that Michael is the angel responsible for the angelic well being of the heavenly realms. It has been recorded that the Archangel Lucifer who attempted a coup, or takeover in the Heavens, was finally overthrown and hurled from the Heavens by this high-ranking Archangel. Michael and his angelic helpers finally restored order in the angelic kingdom and by so doing protected the Throne of the Divine Creator God from 'a take-over-bid' by Lucifer.

In light of the warfare that existed in the angelic ranks and also within the heavens, the stand that Michael took along with loyal legions of angelic beings, set the world stage for all mankind to decide whether to choose the path of evil or goodness. The incident that did take place between Lucifer and Michael and their followers reminded us not only of this scene, as it was recorded in the sacred books of the Bible, but to make a firm stand whether we choose to follow evil or good. The fight between Michael and Lucifer is said to represent the forces of 'light and darkness' which is as evident in our world today as it was then.

Message from Michael:

Open your heart to receive the love of all 'Loves.' I am your helper and want to walk with you each and every step of your journey as well as directing you in your chosen career path. My aim for you is to lead you towards the light. I know this light, as it is my inspiration to chose rightfully to obey- to love- to serve my God.

I don't come to unsettle you but to empower you to believe that what you experience here on Earth is transitory and will not defeat your aspirations. Believe that through all of life's hurts and disappointments there is hope. My ambitions for you are to connect with you in your sacred space and take you by the hand to meet the divine that is already within you. Yes, it is all around you; even the air that you breathe is filled with angelic life force energy. You may not see my angelic helpers, or me but we are here and we want to assist you in every way possible. But first, you have to ask us to come into your heart – your mind – you're thinking. Then we can embrace you lovingly and unconditionally. Our mission is to work for you – with you – and through you!

You are a 'son and daughter of God.' The Divine Creator God who has always loved you created you as a love child. From the moment of your inception through conception, you were cherished and loved. Believe this and you will hear the sacred voices speak to you spirit / your soul. Open your heart to God's love and permit me to come and assist you achieve your 'individual greatness' that will forever bless you as well as others. Permit me to show you the different ways that you can embrace 'divine love' and hear your God speak to you through the elements – the beautiful landscapes and wildlife. My helpers are gathered all around you – listen carefully and attentively and you will hear. Yes, you will also see us and eventually embrace the 'divine' within you. Remember, you are an 'Earth Angel' and together you and I can change the world and make it a safer place for all mankind to behold the face of their God.

If you have difficulty hearing and receiving my message believe in one thing! You are dearly Loved!" Whatever may or will happen to you, you are surrounded by many unseen helpers of the angelic realms. Don't wait for a problem to happen – summon my help today!

2. **Archangel Melchizedek***:* or better named the 'Angel of the Divine Presence.' He was considered like Michael as a high-ranking angel who took the human form to do the work of the Creator God. Sacred Scholars and Angelologists have each accounted in detail that it was Melchizedek who delivered God's Covenant to Abraham In the Catholic Church, when a priest is being ordained into the priesthood the sacred rites of the priest's ordination ceremony clearly states, " You shall be a priest according to the Order of Melchizedek."

Message from Archangel Melchizedek.

I bring you the healing love and power of all angels! Regardless of what is happening in our troubled world, good (Positive) always triumphs over the evil forces (Negative energy). It is worth remembering that what you throw into the Universe – it will come back to you! If you throw out hate – expect hate to be thrown back at you. Reflect – Pray – Be Still and know that wherever you are you are in the presence of our God and the angels of the Four Spheres.

Living in the modern world has its rewards as well as its failures. My presence in the 'Angel Peace Garden' or sacred oasis, is to assist you in achieving wholeness and completeness in your relationships with others. If you are searching for a partner who is of like mind, then know that I am here and believe in what I share with you that when you ask for my help I will come to your rescue immediately. However, unless you ask specifically for my help I cannot intervene or interfere in your life's journey.

It is not good for man/woman to be alone and isolated here on Earth. We need the support love and friendship from soul-mates who will accept us unconditionally and unreservedly regardless of our sexuality, disabilities, or even our religious beliefs. I see you not as a stranger but as a soul-mate seeking the integrity of the divine within you. One of my main responsibilities in the Celestial Magic Placement Square is to support those who are married – who are seeking a life partner – those who may have separated from their partner. I aim to empower the discouraged to receive encouragement and solace during those times when all may seem lost! Modern man/woman have created a new set of values where they can inadvertently create problems in their relationships that would seem on the surface to be insurmountable. There is a disregard for the sanctity of life – of love commitments – of sharing in absolute togetherness with trust, respect, dignity and loyalty for the partners. There is a swing towards being unfaithful in marriage. If we make a commitment to live in a loving partnership with another, regardless of sexual orientation we must be aware that the honeymoon period is not meant to last the entire lifespan of that relationship. When serious problems raise their ugly heads, instead of leaving one's partner and seeking solace in the arms of another we should reflect on what 'marriage' actually means for the survival of that relationship. It is so easy to walk away and forfeit the responsibilities and duties of one's sacred promises to love, respect, support, nurture, encourage and commit one's life to another! These and other associated marital, relationship problems can be resolved without destroying the dignity and self-respect of one's partner. I am here to assist you achieve harmony and unity in that commitment. It is so easy to blame another for one's own mistakes and perpetuate the cycle of hate. It takes a mature person to stop and seek stillness and listen to the sacred voices in the quietness of the moment. It takes divine intervention to empower you to safeguard and protect as well as nurture and sustain one's marriage / partnerships with one's soul mate. You are not an 'island.' You are a member of the human race and a brother /sister of the divine. You are the presence of something richer and greater than the problems that seek to destroy and overthrow the divine life within you!

3. Archangel Uriel: Means "The Fire of God". Uriel is ranked as a Seraph, an Angel of high rank. Angelologists have given a clear description of what Uriel's other titles and names that best describe his favour in the heavenly realms. They are,' Regent of the Sun- Flame of God – Archangel of Salvation.'

Uriel is perceived by Sacred Scholars and Angelologists as being the 'sharpest sighted angelic spirit of all angels in Heaven.

Message from Archangel Uriel.

I am your support when all may seem hopeless!My role and assigned angelic responsibility in the 'sacred angel peace garden,' is to open doors for those who feel prisoners in their oasis. I come with many gifts that will liberate your spirit. Up until now, you haven't asked for my angelic wisdom or assistance! I am here just waiting on your invitation to seek you out and deliver the Love of the angels and our God.

One specific concern of my involvement in the heavenly realms is to support all families, particularly those who are in turmoil – those searching for missing members of their family – family members who have been deeply hurt by either sexual abuse, violence, physical, mental and psychological cruelty.

In the heavens I belong to the family of the 'angelic realm,' serving our Creator God on your behalf! I come to you and all families in love and wish for your personal happiness to be complete at every level of your existence. I am not referring to passing happiness that the world accepts as 'real happiness.' What I am referring to is inner peace and joy that makes you fully complete and joyous in your relationships within your family network. Family means shared togetherness of the joys as well as the sorrows that make us who we are as people. The happiness that I refer to is eternal happiness the kind that this world cannot fully understand or comprehend. True, lasting happiness is achieved when we are in unison with our selves and with the members of our family. Our society today is geared to following the every whim and fancy that takes one! Some of you are led by the nose, just like a bull with a ring attached to its nose. We are unable to make positive choices that will generate inner happiness and fulfilment. Could the reason for this be because you are sometimes weak and lacking real conviction befitting a child of the Creator God? Don't fret! All is not lost. You are not alone in your search for fellowship, freedom, contentment and belonging.

I hope to open the eyes of your spirit by unlocking the chains that are around your tired, weary heart. These chains have stifled your very being and have prevented you from being "You." Let me help you right now to experience the real inner joys of spirit! This unique joy will saturate your very soul – spirit life and empower you to be who you are meant to be! You are not to be a slave to the trends of the modern world! Forget about the fashions and trends that may set you above your neighbour and leave you feeling a sense of false insecurity. You may well find that you have already become arrogant, complacent, self sufficient, self-indulgent and unbearable to live with within a family. Let me help you escape from these false gods. Gods that rob you of

your dignity as a fellow human being that is worthy of respect and kindness; warmth, love and inner beauty that we can see. What does it matter what the world, or society thinks of you! Why loose out and be abandoned by those who are inwardly jealous of what you have achieved. Are they more worthy of your affection? No!

Come with me and let me share with you the real joys of life and love. Let me show you a different way that has stood the test of time. This way is easy to follow and getting there doesn't involve hardship or financial insecurity. Just ask me to come and assist you in your quest for inner fulfilment and spiritual contentment that will generate a positive response from within and around your sacred oasis.

I am here to enable those of you who have no 'earth family' (brothers and sisters) to encourage and motivate you achieve your full potential! I will lead you to your new family of soul seekers searching out the divine and angelic life force energy that fulfils and satisfies us at every level of our etheric being. Though you may seem alone in this world, yet, you are never alone when you embrace the divine in your sacred oasis. You are surrounded by a myriad of angels and divine beings. You only have to connect to the angelic realm through our frequency. We are accessible twenty-four hours a day, seven days a week; fifty-two weeks of eternity. When you ask me to help you I am already in your 'master plan.' Remember, that I cannot help you unless you first ask! I respect your free will and because of this, I can only come when summoned. When I do come to you I assure you that you will experience a joy this world cannot or will not understand, even comprehend! My promise to you today is that I will take you by the hand and lead you to places that will satisfy your spirit to the point of ecstasy. I will lead you into the presence of the Divine God who made you in his/her image and likeness! You will know what it is to be a valued member of a loving family.

4. ***Archangel Moroni***: Known as the 'Angel of Light'. *Angelologists have said that Moroni appeared to Joseph Smith in 1823 in the USA and known as the Angel of the Latter Day Saints (Mormons). According to several experts, it has been said of Moroni that when he appeared to John Smith, the face of Moroni was as a "Being of Light with a face resembling lightening."*

Message from Archangel Moroni.

"Blessed are those who are poor in spirit, for theirs is indeed the kingdom of heaven." I want you to listen very carefully to what I am telling you now- that will hopefully benefit your entire life and those around you.

My assigned areas of responsibility within the Angel Bagua – Magic Placement Square is concerned with 'wealth.' Modern man say you are

what you eat and known by what you wear! I say to you that you are none of these in the eyes of the angelic realms or before the Creator God who made you! You are a 'Child of the Divine God' whose father is a millionaire! Do you believe this? Possibly not, or maybe you are feeling somewhat threatened by the statement that your 'Father is a millionaire.' I am not referring to your natural father. I am referring only to your Heavenly Father – the loving God who created you as a unique individual representing divine ethereal love here on Earth.

Wealth is usually perceived by most as that referring to cash – money – dollars – riches! I perceive wealth not as any of these but as that rare and precious gift that has no price tag. It is like a rare and precious pearl and when found you take it home and value it by caring for it and restoring it to its former glory and beauty. You don't squander it or abuse it by being careless and foolish. Your spirit / soul is just like that precious pearl but much more valuable.

I want you to enter your sacred angel peace garden and be aware that you are in the presence of the angelic realms and standing before your God. The earth you are standing on is no ordinary earth. Believe me when I share with you that you are standing on sacred ground. It is a sad and disturbing fact that too often man disregards the sanctity of life. Poverty is man inflicted and not God created! Those who are poor and devoid of sufficient means to live on for their survival are the unfortunate victims of 'man's in humanity to man.' It is not the Creator's wish to see his children die of starvation and poverty. There is a sufficient amount of food and grain to feed the entire world twice over! The inequalities are as a direct result of greed and the power to control. We can correct these injustices and inequalities through a more honest distribution and supply of the Earth's food stores. It is the will of the Creator that all mankind access the universal wealth that is there in abundance for one and all! Your needs are already known to us but you do not ask – or you don't know how to access the wealth of the angels and your God. It is not evil to be rich or to have acquired your financial wealth honourably. However, if you have acquired your wealth dishonourably through unlawful means or on the backs of the 'poor,' then to have engaged in such practices is evil! You will never inherit the 'wealth' of eternity until you amend or change your ways. As on Earth, you have Banks and financial institutions that invest your savings. So it is here in the Heavenly city. We have 'angel bankers' who invest the talents and skills of the Creator's work force and generate positive results through these wise and prudent investments. I ask you to be aware of the angel bankers and ask them to assist you to benefit from their heavenly

administrations. They won't give you the numbers for a lottery win, but they will certainly give to you a percentage of your low income to help you stay healthy and live a meaningful life. All you have to do is to ask – believe- trust- and accept in love. Remember, your heavenly Father who is the supreme God of all life force energies on Earth is a beneficent God who wants to share the wealth of the heavenly kingdoms with you today.

6. ***Archangel Israfael: Known as the 'Burning One'.*** *According to Angelologists, Israfael is said to have paved the way for Gabriel by serving for three years as a companion to Mohammed, whom he had originally initiated as a prophet.*

In the Islamic version of the story of Genesis account of Adam's creation, Allah sends Israfael, Gabriel, Michael and Azrael – the Angel of Death – out on a mission to fetch the seven handfuls of dust needed to make humanity's progenitor. According to legend, only Azrael returned successful.

Israfael is described as the 'four-winged angel'. Israfael is reported in sightings whose 'heart strings are a lute, and who has the sweetest voice of all God's creatures.' It is said that this wonderful Archangel sings God's praises in a thousand different tongues.

Israfael is the Patron of entertainers and Artists.

Again it has been said of Israfael, that when the end of the world finally arrives, he will descend to Earth and stand on the Holy Rock in Jerusalem and blow the sacred trumpet that will awaken all the dead from their slumber and summon all who have ever lived to come and meet their judgement. Angelologists have said of Israfael that he looks into Hell three times during each day and night he is stricken with great grief that makes him weep to the point of flooding the Earth with his tears. The torment that he sees in Hell is said to be so great that it leaves him sad for all mankind who choose to ignore the love of God.

Message from Archangel Israfael.

Enlightenment comes from knowledge and knowledge comes through being wise. Wisdom is the result of listening to the inner voices of the divine speaking 'words of wisdom and instruction' through the elements and the angelic servers in and around you. My assignment in the angel peace garden as depicted in the 'Magic Placement Square,' is to help you achieve positive or 'Chi' energy in your sacred angel peace oasis.

Silence is the sister of the Divine! It is only in the silence and stillness of our sacred oasis that we can engage with the divine. Noise, upheaval, restlessness, inner disquiet are antagonists to acquiring chi energy in our lives. To live the 'spiritual life' and nurture our spirit we are encouraged to take time out to reflect and listen to the sacred inner voices of spirit.

We live in a wonderful and beautiful world that was created by the Creator for our enjoyment as well as pleasure. There is excitement and great expectations in the faces of everyone! However, the pull of the world usually saps our energy and at best, we are left isolated and feeling bereft of spiritual nourishment. We become the victims of our own undoing! Our exposure to excess pleasure and excitement, late nights and inadequate respite leaves us impoverished in every sense of the word! We become victims of our own undoing / greed and survival is for the fittest with the weak falling in their droves. You end up being led by the nose through the 'flesh-pots of Egypt,' and instead of rejoicing in what is beautiful and glorious you become sad and dispirited people like 'aliens' from another planet. You are like a house built on sand – it collapses when the storms come and blast its very foundations into oblivion! Why do you allow this?

We are made of three key elements, mind-body-spirit. We cannot ignore one at the sole expense of the other element. We are obliged to safeguard each key component by ensuring a daily diet that will sustain our spirit and help us maintain an 'even balance.' When you ignore the spirit in favour of the mind or body, you incur the wrath of nature and the elements of spirit. Your lives are not meant to live in chaos or disharmony but in unison of spirit in close fellowship with the elements and alive to your surroundings.

Acquiring 'chi' is achievable and accessible! You must make time and do a 'stock check' so as to replenish your spiritual life with the essential ingredients that will empower you to connect with your divinity as well as your spirit. When you involve a garden designer to come and plan your sacred oasis you listen carefully to their advice and despite the financial outlay, you are prepared to make the necessary sacrifices to achieve your 'dream garden.' So it is with accessing inner peace and harmony within yourself. Spiritual values are essential for your survival in the modern world. To be successful in the market place and hold onto that creative job of yours you must make sacrifices for your personal success! So it is with your interior life of spirit. You have to set aside time each and every day to make that all-important connection between you and your God; you and the angelic realms. It is not as difficult as you might imagine! It involves time and effort of equal proportions. Because you live in a busy world that makes demands upon your physical as well as your spiritual-life, you have

to be aware that you will have to prioritise and avoid the fast lane if you are to succeed in the spiritual –interior life. What you put into your spiritual life will return dividends that will take you to a higher plane of spiritual enlightenment or 'nirvana.'

Nirvana is not out there! It is here in the present and by adopting changes to your present lifestyle, you will access the benefits of 'chi' positive energy in yourself. I walk beside you daily and I am in the whisper of unspoken words that inspire you to reach out and touch the divine in creation. You are divine and because you are made up of spirit-energies you need to spend time each day alone with me and with your God. Rejoice and be glad because you are almost there! Now, walk the rest of the journey with me and experience the real lasting joys of inner-bliss in the presence of the divine

7. ***Archangel Raziel:*** *The name literally means,* ***"Secret of the Creator God," and belongs to the Celestial Choir of the Cherubim.*** *It is said that Raziel is an angel of the secret regions and Chief of the 'Supreme Mysteries.'(1.500 keys to the mysteries of Heaven). He is the patron of the first human – Adam and it is said that he stands at the veil separating God from creation and records everything said at the Throne of God. Raziel is the author of the Book called the Tome where Noah gained his information to build the Ark.*

Raziel is recognised by a yellow aura surrounding his angelic appearance. It is said that if you were to see him he would appear tall showing his large wings that are sky blue in colour. He is the guardian of originality, pure ideas and dreams. Known to be exceptionally helpful and supportive in clarification of certain truths surrounding confusion as well as certain myths relating to the occult in the universe. Raziel understands the power, speed and flow of electrical energy systems in the universe. Raziel is seen as a high ranking angel and is perceived within the angelic realm as being a senior angel we would call today as a 'Boss Angel.'

Messages from Archangel Raziel.

I am the Archangel Raziel and my role is to empower you to walk humbly in reverence with us and thereby access the ethereal benefits and divine riches freely available to those who seek divine enlightenment. I am your advocate and messenger sent to you from our Creator God who is keen that you make contact and benefit from life here on Earth. Your angel sacred peace garden / sacred oasis is no ordinary place! Here in our sacred garden you will embrace the divine and benefit from that connectedness. All you have to do is be still – be aware – rejoice and know that in the secret

recesses of this sacred oasis we are present waiting for you to come and join us. Yes, we may be unseen to the naked eye, but please don't fear! We are all around you working tirelessly and effortlessly on your behalf.

My specific area of support that I can offer you is to share with you what I do for you and others. My job description is to safeguard 'benefactors' and help you benefit from the blessings given freely by benefactors to those who are in need of support. The word benefactor should not be merely perceived as someone who gives 'charity' to the less fortunate. There are different types of benefactors who wait to give generously of their gifts to enhance your faith-spiritual journey. In most cases, our benefactors remain 'silent-sleeping-partners.' They respond when I summon their help on your behalf.

Situated in the North West section of the Placement Square Benefactors range from support from our angels, members of your family; distant relations now in spirit, or soul light seekers who have heard or seen your plight and have volunteered to help you in your time of disquiet or trouble! When you approach me personally I already know your thoughts and have already prepared an 'action-plan' to remedy your plight. Seek and you will find the healing beneficial support from your God through the angelic realms and spirit world. Unless you come and ask you will never know what surprises are in store for you.

As a servant messenger of the most High-God, I know no obstacles or agenda that could separate my love for you right now. Regardless of where you have travelled to seek enlightenment be aware of those who profess to be agents of the Divine God! The world is filled with many 'false prophets' who claim to know the answer to your situation. I ask that you exercise caution and seek the gift of discernment that will help you recognise these false prophets and steer clear of them!

8. ***Archangel Raphael: The name means, "God Has Healed."*** *Raphael is a senior archangel and one who is given the sole responsibility for the healing of all God's people and of the entire Universe. There are many examples of Raphael's healing ministry recorded in the sacred books of all major world religions.Angelologists have said that Raphael is said to be one of the most loved of all the angels in the heavens. Images of Raphael are still being painted by artists today.*

There is a legend that when Solomon prayed to God for aid in building the temple in Jerusalem, Raphael personally delivered the gift of a magic ring that had sacred powers to overcome demon spirits.

Messages from Archangel Raphael

I am the Archangel Raphael and I represent the healing power of the living God who desires that you be free of all ills that separate your spirit from the divine! I am a servant of the Creator God of all the living and I am here to be your servant in those times of anxiety. I bring you the love from the God who made you in love and I share with you the energy of all here in the angelic realms of the Fourth Spheres of angelic servers.

My specific role in the Angel Placement Square and Bagua is Archangel Prince of the West with a responsibility for all children of the Universe. You are called to be 'childlike' and not childish! Children have a rare quality of seeing through the mind-games and agendas that adults use to get their own way. Regrettably, children have been exploited and abused by adults over the centuries and it is my responsibility to ensure that they are protected. My angelic helpers work best when they have you and the adult population of the world on board. Sadly, man's inhumanity to children has greatly saddened me and I now need your support to challenge society to rethink their beliefs and values towards all children.

I come in love and with the healing energy of a loving, generous God. You too are loved and accepted as a valued member of the human family. When you call on me I will come and assist you in whatever circumstances that you may be in right now. Your worries, fears and battles are mine too! Know that I am with you even in your darkest hours and am there walking close beside you through it all.

Healing comes in many different ways. Yes, there is immediate healing known as ' a miracle.' There is healing that is a slow, gradual process that appears to take forever. Often when you ask for a specific healing for a physical problem and there appears to be no direct answer to your requests, the healing may have been directed to another area that is in need of divine healing! Healing can come to you in many different ways and through a variety of practitioners. Divine healing touches the lives of many souls that desperately need healing. For example, divine healing often comes through the expertise of the surgeon; the Palliative care nurse specialist; the Dentist; the healing group in your local church. There is direct healing and there is indirect healing that releases us from the negative energies that cripple your mind – your physical body – your emotional and spiritual life.

In the complexities of life, often we are not meant to know the answers to everything but seek inner calm through quiet reflective stillness and prayer in our sacred oasis. When you raise your mind and heart towards the divine God who made you angels are immediately sent to comfort you in

your trials. If there is a serious health problem then I am told of this and am ready to assist you through the pitfalls. Remember, prayers said either to God the Healer, or directed to one of the angels is never ignored! Your prayers for divine assistance are heard and answered in the ways that are best for you. We can see the whole picture whereas you can only see the immediate problem which often blinds you to the real truth of life's great mystery, Always be assured that whenever you summon the support of the angelic realms help is given immediately. Remember the poem about the 'Footprints' in the sand? Be of good courage and never despair when the trials of life hit home causing you to waver. I am here with you through it all! You are not alone! Though you may feel that you are alone – rest awhile and believe that here in the calling out in your distress – I am right beside you. I am in the air that you breathe; the warmth of the sun's rays is the embodiment of my wings surrounding you. Please do not become discouraged if you don't experience immediately! There is a genuine reason and through quiet stillness in your sacred space you will be told everything you need to know.

9. **The Archangel Ariel: Whose *name means 'Lion of God,' and according to Angelologists as one of the seven princes who rule the waters of the Earth.*** Ariel is one of the over lighting angels that is recorded in several of the world's 'Holy Books'.

The Archangel Ariel is a high ranking angel and a member of the Thrones who are associated with the nine choirs of angels. The Archangel Raphael and angel Ariel have been recorded as being a healing partnership by in curing disease and helping alleviate the sufferings of all mankind.

Messages from Archangel Ariel:

I am the Archangel Ariel and my presence is everywhere but more so in the North Eastern area of your angel peace garden. I am assigned with a specific responsibility to raise awareness about developing and nurturing your personal relationships with your Creator God – your higher-self – your destiny and about the meaning and purpose of why you are here on Earth.

I represent the spirit of knowledge and how you as an individual can acquire knowledge about yourself – your relationships with the divine and others. Knowledge is essential if you are to succeed in this life's plane. Without having developed a common sensed approach to knowledge and all matters appertaining to its inner riches and spiritual values you will loose out on life's destiny for your own achievements. To go through life with limited knowledge of survival you will surely fail miserably in your

life's work and achievements. Ignorance is not acceptable and you cannot use the 'excuse card' to avoid accessing knowledge.

Yes, there are different types of knowledge and here I shall concentrate not on academic knowledge but on a 'common sensed' approach to understanding why you were born and what purposes we have for you as a child of God on this Earth plane. You have to take time out from your hectic schedules and listen to the still voice in silence. It is unfashionable to pray, or is it? You are made of up different parts that make you what you really are! If you deny your physical body food it will die from starvation. This is not good but foolish. If you eat sensibly you will live a long and healthy life and hopefully you will be content and happy! However, if you fail to satisfy your interior life – spirit- then you will stagnate and drift aimlessly throughout life. You will not live but only exist as an unfulfilled human being that has lost sight of your goal and purpose of being here. Your interior life of spirit is as important for your survival in the rat race we call modern society. Society is forever pointing the finger at God as to why he permits disasters to strike the family of man. It is not God who is guilty of the gross miscarriages of justices but the human race. What can you expect when mankind shuts the door to divine love and says we don't want to know!

Society says no to the Creator's love. Governments say no to God's healing and protective love. Most business say no to divine love. Do you say no to this all embracing, unconditional love too? The reason why you and the rest of mankind are unfulfilled and satisfied with life is because you find it 'unfashionable' to pray and deny yourself the pleasures of experiencing the real riches and joys of living a spirit-filled life of love. The reason mankind is disillusioned with living life on Earth today is because of a lack of knowledge about all matters divine. Desolate is the world right now because you fail to comprehend or understand the real meaning of love- God's Love – the Creator's love – angels love for you where you are at right now. Open you heart and your mind to receive love and thereby acquire knowledge that will transform your life for all eternity. Let your interior spirit experience this wonderful sacred experience of connecting the two spirits – yours with the Divine Creator God. If and when you decide to embrace angelic love you will fly like a bird and experience real joy that is selfless, forgiving, enduring for all time.

10. **The Archangel Gabriel:** ***Whose name means, "God is my strength," as well as known as the 'heavenly awakener.'*** It was Gabriel who appeared to Mary at her Annunciation, to announce that she would conceive and bear a son

– the Son of God. It has also been recorded by Sacred Scholars that Gabriel appeared to Mary's cousin Elizabeth to inform her that she, too, would bear a son who would be called, 'John The Baptist.'

Muslims believe that Gabriel is the Spirit of Truth who dictated the Koran to the Prophet Mohammed. In Jewish traditions, it is believed that it was Gabriel who parted the waters of the Red Sea so that the Hebrews could escape from the soldiers of the infamous Pharaoh.

Messages from Archangel Gabriel:

I am Gabriel the Archangel of the South and I greet you in the name of all loves – the divine God who loves me with the very same love that God loves you! My sharing with you now is fuelled by my interest in you and your future destiny as a co creator of the same divine God who loves everything that was created in love. I am assigned to protect and nurture you and empower you to benefit from your regular contacts with the angelic realms in your sacred angel peace garden / oasis. Part of my remit is to assist you reach your full potential and thereby use your talents to glorify the spirit of living love within you before men. I have been identified as a go-between in difficult situations as well as being made Patron of communications globally. My task in the sacred angel peace garden is to show you how you too can be recognised as a unique individual especially chosen and loved. Your needs and want checklist can go on forever and a day! However, there is one particular area of your life that is still unfulfilled and this has left you feeling empty and at times lonely. We are all famous before the Creator God who made us in their image and likeness. Through my daily involvement in the Angel Bagua and Healing Trigram I am responsible for facilitating changes in your life that will open doors for your happiness. Fame when it comes can cost us our life's work even our dignity if we are not prepared for its successes. Recognition for our hard-earned achievements in either the work place or in our personal lives is laudable and commendable before men. But we are to be on our guard against the sinister forces of man's pride and arrogance for fear we get too 'big-headed,' and loose everything we have worked hard for in this life. You know what I am trying to share with you regarding the downside to fame. It is sad when one minute a famous person who has commanded the applause and respect of the world stage and suddenly falls from grace in the public eye. It is equally disturbing to read about certain members of society who achieve their greatness on the backs of the poor! Because you live in a modern world that at best has lost sight of the spiritual values that make you what you are today it is disturbing to receive notice of the lengths that man will go to so as to keep his fame, or good reputation intact. If you dabble with evil forces be assured that what you through at others the same will inevitably come back on you

and take your reputation leaving you in tatters. Many a great person has courted the world's stage and fallen flat on their faces only to discover to their detriment that their friends were not really genuine but 'fair weather friends.' What brings fame to you is an open trusting nature that recognises the self-worth of each and every individual regardless of their material wealth or fame. If you can see the face of your Creator God in the faces of ordinary men and women then and only then have you become famous before your God. Then you will experience the real friendship of the angels and know what it is to have genuine fame in your life. Are you ready to forfeit the spiritual values for earthly values and loose out altogether? You are indeed a wise person who can see through the folly of courting false Gods and false hopes and dreams that will come to nothing. Be wise and seek first the kingdom of your God and the angels and all else will be given to you in abundance. Knowing such a treasure is there for the asking is indeed fame without the hardships of having to loose your spirit – your soul in the race.

The Archangel Metatron: ***Whose name means "One who occupies the throne next to the Throne of God.***" He is seen as the Liberating Angel who wrestled with Jacob. According to several Jewish mystics, Metatron came to hold the highest rank of angels despite no reference to this in Sacred Scriptures! Another of his titles are, Chancellor of Heaven, King of the Angels, Highest Power of Abundance, the Supreme Angel of Death, the Twin Brother of Angel Sandalphan; Keeper of the Sacred Scrolls and is overseer of the Planet Uranus. According to Angelologists, Metatron is said to have lived on Earth as the Prophet Enoch, who was taken up into Heaven and transformed into an 'angel of fire,' with thirty-six pairs of wings. Metatron is said to have been the angel who stopped Abraham sacrificing his son Isaac. It is also mentioned in Jewish folklore that it was Metatron who led the Hebrews through the wilderness for some forty years.

Messages from Metatron:

I am the Archangel Metatron who speaks to your higher self in love and with the blessings of the most high Creator God who has assigned the duties and responsibilities of the Angel Bagua, Healing Trigram and Celestial Placement Square. These sacred tools are no ordinary tools that you can pick up and drop whenever the fancy takes you. They are not disposable like surgical instruments that a surgeon disposes of after a surgical procedure. They are the tools that will facilitate a connection with your Creator through angelic involvement in your sacred oasis. You can use these tools anywhere…they don't have to be used especially in the garden. Yes, they were designed for creating an angel sacred peace garden but you can equally apply the

principles of the angel Bagua in your home. My main role in all of this is to act as an overseer who knows when to involve not just the services of one Archangel but when appropriate involve the services of many angels who are available to help you achieve spiritual enlightenment and achieve your goals. Although I have been portrayed as the greatest angel that has ever existed yet I am afforded the same love and spiritual blessings that are now freely available to you today. The Creator God who loves me also loves you as an equal to me. In our kingdom God has no favourites but accepts and loves all of his angels with the same intensity as God loves you where you are at right now. This is worth some reflection and you need to fully comprehend what this means for you. I can empathise with you in your plight and daily struggles to regain control of your life in the midst of so much adversity and conflict. The world is so confused and its inhabitants are mostly chasing their tails or fighting against the winds of change. I once lived among God's people as a responsible citizen but like you I was misunderstood for standing up for integrity and justice including 'fair play' for all of God's people. I lived many centuries ago but believe me when I tell you that life on Earth is no different now as it was in my time. Man is still searching for the impossible dreams and continually frustrated by his meaningless existence. I bring you an offer of eternal life through making the necessary changes that are relevant in your faith – spiritual journey towards the divine. I am here to show you how you can access that divine life by doing ordinary things extraordinarily well with the support of myself by your side. I am drawn to you to empower you to 'rise up' and go free from the ravages of a wasted life. Seek inner peace and joy here right now. Open your lives to receive the breath of the angel's breath. Open your eyes of spirit and behold the greatest love story ever told about you and the God who loved you from the beginning of infinite time. The 'Divine Blueprint' as outlined in the angel Bagua is about making peace with your higher self and experiencing the inner completeness that this brings to you. This transformation won't cost you a penny! To experience a complete change of image costs the earth! Look at those who cannot accept themselves and live like 'peter pans' forever trying this new face lift and that tuck of excess fat..... It costs and they pay dearly for within the false smiles there is a longing to be loved and accepted as they were before they had radical surgery! Here in this city of eternal love and angelic-light energy we don't know fear, hate, guilt, shame, despair as you do on Earth. In fact we don't fully understand why on Earth you cannot understand that life there is momentary. If you are experiencing deep despair or that inner peace and joy is beyond your physical grasp – fear not! I am there along side you in your present plight. I was assigned to help you achieve all that you ever dreamed and hoped for in this life. But first, you have to take time out and reflect on where you are going and what it is that you actually wish for yourself. When you sense that all around you seems hopeless and you are feeling helpless, fear not! I come not as a thief in the night but as a messenger of the Divine Creator God who loves you and I as equals. Remember that when you hear others say that we have no need of God but we will engage with the angels be aware that they represent not the 'Light' but the dark side! From the beginning of time there have always been false prophets who convincingly try to confuse God's chosen people. I use the word chosen not to reflect on the Jewish nation but to state that those who embrace the "Universal Life / Light force angelic energy" embrace the divine God who created you and me! I ask you to discern the words and instructions from those who say they represent the light. Put them to the test! Never accept their words as gospel but reflect on them and what they, the false prophets, are telling you to do. Be aware and be on your guard for the thief of God is alive and active and will use every despicable means to confuse you and lead you from the real truth. Seek out the wisdom of all holy men and women and reflect on their teachings in your heart. I am Metatron, servant of the most high God who loves you with a love this world does not fully understand or comprehend. Rejoice and know that I am here together with the entire angelic host at your disposal so that you will never feel alone or rejected. Remember that all we ask of you is that you will walk humbly before your God and seek only the universal life / light force angelic energies that are in abundance in your sacred oasis /angel peace garden.

Firstly, I would like to share my personal thoughts about the 'Boss' Archangel who is the overseer of all that transpires within the angel sacred peace garden. This angel is no ordinary angel! He is the Archangel Metatron and it is alleged that unlike ordinary angels who have one pair of wings, Metatron has 36 pairs of angelic wings with a wingspan of several hundred feet in diameter.

Metatron is referred to as ' the Chancellor of Heaven.' He is considered to be of considerable importance in the angelic realms. Angelologists are in agreement that Metatron is considered greater than Michael and Gabriel.

Metatron, whose name means 'God in Man.' Angelologists believe that Metatron is the tallest angel, whose face is described as resembling the blazing sun with a dazzling appearance that prevents man looking into his eyes. Metatron radiates the divine presence wherever he goes and when we encounter his presence we sense a rekindling of the divine within our souls / spirit. Metatron's key responsibilities as Chancellor of Heaven involves supporting and sustaining all mankind regardless of our diversity. He holds the key to the eternal kingdom linking man with everything that is associated with the divine! In essence, this worthy Archangel is always one step ahead of mankind by facilitating and empowering each of us to connect with our God. He breathes the divine life force energy into our very souls encouraging us to respond in triumphant praise by accepting and recognising that we are sons and daughters of the 'Divine God/dess.'

Metatron is the 'hound of heaven' searching out the lost souls so that they can behold the face of the Creator. When we call on him we are never disappointed with the results!

In March 2003 I received a beautiful painting of the Archangel Metatron with a simple message. His message to me on 17th March 2003 still holds true for me. It reads: " Given to Sean Jude Bradley to heal souls broken by man in ignorance and pain."

Messages from the Archangels arrived on 29th September 2000 (Feast of the Archangel Princes).

Feedback from our student therapists to Sean's CD Working With our Angels:

Angels are divine messengers of God ever present, from the beginning of time. They are ever present in our world, to guide, protect, direct mankind. Angels range from the Nature beings, elementals, divas –they mature through the ranks to Choirs of angels, Virtues, Powers, Dominations, Seraphim, Cherubim and the Archangels.

There are angels for the realms of Earth, fire, water and air, all found in nature. In order for man to contact angels, he should do so in a spirit of reverence and respect, invoking, asking and inviting them to come from all 4 points of the compass.

Man should, at this time remain quiet, respectful and open to whatever messages the angels may give, i.e. Behold, Hold, Enfold and Listen, in a spirit of humility and reverence.

Notice should be taken of any signs denoting the presence of angels, e.g. in touch, smell, taste, visions, that man may receive. By being receptive, and open to the messages, man can then become a channel, through which divine unconditional love may pass to the client in the process of therapeutic channelling.

At the end of communication with our angels, we give thanks to them for their presence, in the realisation we may live in a spirit of expectancy, being able to call upon them all the time.

We may call for them to go before us in our situations, so peace, harmony and calm may be apparent, whatever the situation may be in our lives at that moment.

We may ask our angel to give direction to the individuals in our lives, through them speaking to the individuals guardian angel, so that conflict may be resolved, to the mutual benefit of all concerned.

In the presence of our angels, we can let go and let God be, being reassured, that they have an influence over us, as long as we are open to their call and presence in our lives.

Keywords for the assignment are:- expectancy –trust –knowledge is power and synchronicity. **Theresa D (August '04)**

"Behold I send an Angel before you!" This is the first thing that I picked up from the recording; this one sentence speaks volumes to me. The angels are God's messengers and through them He guides us, guards us and showers us with His infinite love. To me, Angels are the arms of

God, they wrap themselves around us when we are feeling alone, when we cry out for help, it is the Angels who answer our call.
Angels come in all forms, both Heavenly, and Earthly. Since becoming aware of the Angels I find little white feathers everywhere, this is one of the signs that the Angels are around us. I've encountered people and even pets who I am sure are Angels. I've had visions of Angels in all colours, gold, silver, blue, purple, brilliant white light, huge angels, 7 or 8 feet tall, and tiny angels only 2 or 3 inches in size, but they all have one thing in common, they come with unconditional love. Mostly they are invisible, but just as real as the life force that runs through us.

There are 3 known orders of angelic beings:

The 1st Choir –are the Seraphim, Cherubim and Thrones.

The 2nd Choir –are the Dominions, Virtues and Powers.

The 3rd Choir- are the Principalities, the Archangels and the angels.

There is also a 4th Sphere of angelic beings known as the Elementals; they are concerned with the 4 Universal Life Force Elements:

The Earth Realm /The Fire realm / The Air realm / The Water realm.

These Elementals are also known as Fairies, Tree Diva's, Crystal Diva's and they live in nature, the flowers, woods and rivers.

Angels are not permitted to interfere with man's free will, we can ask, invite and invoke the Angels to be with us, there is a sacred mantra for the angels, it is: Eee Nu Rah –times 3 and it means "Angels here I am I come to be with you". When you ask for their help be aware of sounds, scents and visions given by them to you.

Angels have been with us since the beginning of Creation, they are instruments of peace and they bring us love and light and walk beside us through our darkest times. The angels arrive at the moment of physical death of the body and lead us home into the Light of God.

We are surrounded by these beautiful Beings from the moment of our birth. We all have a Guardian Angel who has a special name –just ask for the name and listen for the reply –it will be given!

The angels will support us always in our lives; they will guide us and walk beside us in our days ahead. **Cindy C (December '04).**

Angels are messengers of God and are made of ethereal matter (i.e. Spirit). They have existed since the beginning of Creation and they are immortal.
There are 4 orders of Angelic Beings:-

1. Heavenly Counsellors:-
    - Seraphims
    - Cherubims
    - Thrones
2. Heavenly Governors:-
    - Dominions
    - Virtues
    - Powers
3. Messengers:-
    - Principalities
    - Archangels (Michael, Gabriel, Raphael, Uriel, Metatron, etc.
    - *Angels

* Angels are the closest to humanity and are responsible for human affairs. They are our companion angels or Guardian Angels.

4. Nature Waves: responsible for:
    - Earth Realm
    - Fire realm
    - Air Realm
    - Water Realm
    - Animal Kingdom

Angels have been in business since the beginning of Creation. In the Bible, there are 385 references to the existence of angels and their direct involvement with man. Angels light the way for us, they are messengers of God's love for us, they strengthen us, communicate with us; teach us; fight with us-fight for us.

We can become connected with our angels and feel their presence when we are still, calm. Especially when we are in nature, when there is less noise and pollution. We can repay the angels by sending them love.

Angels are not only guardians, they also guide us to greater consciousness; they bring us back to where we came from –to God /Godess. **Angela A (December '04)**

The Angel Bagua and Healing Trigram

The Angel Bagua and Healing Trigram are Divine blueprints for soul seekers as well as for gardeners to use to enable them to work with Archangel Metatron in blessing your sacred space / oasis / garden/ the Earth.

I have created with the angels an Angel Magic Square that you align at your garden's entrance. The square is a divine blueprint for all soul seekers and gardeners to use to enable them to work with Archangel Metatron. The blueprint divides the garden into nine sectors and each sector is aligned to the energies and vibration of an archangel.

The use of the Angel Bagua works closely with the Angels of the Earth Realms; the four elements as well as the angels of the animal kingdom.

Rationale for the specific colours in the Bagua and Placement Square.

The Archangel princes were placed according to the frequency at which they resonate and the direction, i.e. North, South, East, West rather than there associated colour. Neither seems either right or wrong -just different energy needs for different tasks.

Blessings to you Sean: Andromeda 16th April 2004

The Angel Bagua 'Divine Blue-Print'

Nobody was more confused or surprised than myself when I was given the actual 'Divine Blue Print.' Why me? I repeatedly asked myself. It came as a bolt of lightening out of the blue! I am not an artist and my artistic drawing skills are certainly not worth talking about. In fact, if the truth were told, I cannot draw to save my skin! So, the idea, or conceptual diagrams and detailed colour and inspirational pictures that were drawn by my hand were influenced by spirit.

In the weeks that followed I was being prepared for the greatest gift of all. That gift was to receive the presence of my God in the form of a deep abiding love surrounded by a light that was a blinding light energy. To describe this 'energy' is beyond words. In fact, there are no words in the English language that can best describe that wonderful inner joy. This light / presence would wake me up at 3 am each and every morning to behold the presence of angels. Now, I am wakened on a regular basis to come down stairs and be still waiting for our angels to come and share with me their instructions for others; for my work; how best that I can serve the Divine in what I say and do through my servant hood as a co worker of the Divine Creator.

What I was to receive was not something that I was capable of organising or even plotting! The idea or concept of an 'angel sacred peace garden' was not part of my vocabulary. In truth, the 'divine blueprint that was to change the course of my life was as a direct result of Divine intervention.

What really happened in late 1998, may be conceived as being some 'crank' trying to make a few bucks out of those who are gullible to part with their hard earned cash / dollars! I was still totally ignorant of what I was experiencing in terms of the thoughts and creative ideas that were being implanted inside my head. The concept of the 'divine blueprint' was received in my prayer times alone with my Creator God/ess and my angels.

I have never professed to be an artist. My chosen career in life was that of being a qualified nurse. I could never say that I was good at drawing. I would say, however, that my drawings were very much like that of a 5 year old in kindergarten. During those special moments alone with my God/ess and our angels in quiet prayer, I would often sense the need to pick up a pen and spare paper and suddenly my hand would literally take off! I would scribble, draw objects and write words that meant little or nothing at all to me. Yes, my hand held the pen but an unseen force present that guided my hand and my thoughts carried out the actual designs.

When I had completed several of these rather bizarre exercises I would reflect on what I had written and drawn and was totally confused. I didn't understand or comprehend the content of my work. I would sit there quietly mesmerised and repeatedly ask myself what it all meant. The words "Archangel Princes, Bagua, Trigram, sacred colours and angels of Nature," meant nothing to me! I had never heard of Feng Shui. The only element I knew of was that in an electrical kettle that would heat the cold water. In fact, the words 'Magic Square' conjured up something of a superstitious religion or Cult! I was really confused and the only way I could fathom out what these new concepts, ideas meant was to spend longer periods in silence and prayer.

In the December 1999, I was given a gift of a rather beautiful book that explained 'The Principles of Feng Shui.' I was interested to read and see a diagram that resembled my 'divine blueprint.' I was overwhelmed with joy knowing that what I had previously received was not a 'figment of my imagination.' At last, I could make some sense of what I had been entrusted with in 1998. I consider myself to be a mere novice when it comes to understanding the arena of 'alternative therapies.' I guess my previous training as a qualified nurse practitioner for 38 years made me somewhat sceptical as I had encountered several outfits that proclaimed to the local population that, 'they were here to save the world,' so to speak. Or was it my negativity that prevented me from taking on board a new alternative-concept to healthcare delivery!

However, in my new book about Feng Shui and how to use it effectively in your home and garden so as to improve the 'yin and yang' in one's sacred oasis, I was surprised to read that it was 3000 years old! At this point I became somewhat downcast as I sensed that here was a 3000-year-old theory that had stood the test of time and succeeded. I brought my feelings of despair to the angels one morning at 3am and shared with them my confusion and disquiet regarding the Feng Shui Bagua and the 'divine blueprint.' Before I could get my breath, the angelic realm not to make comparisons but seek the light and not dwell too much on what I had read in my Feng Shui book was politely admonishing me. Before daylight graced the early morning skies, the angels of the Nature Realm to accept one very important piece of this jigsaw were tutoring me. It was made very clear to me that angelogy (study of angels) reveals and testifies to the fact that angels precede Feng Shui and all other religions by millions of years. I was also made aware that angels were created in 'the infinity of time.' The angels belonging to the first Three Spheres of angelic servers, or better known as the 'Nine Choirs,' of angels have never experienced birth or death. When the Creator created Angels of the first ' Three Spheres,' they were given the breath of 'divine life' instantly! However, I was later informed that the Fourth Sphere of angels, or better known as angels of the "Nature Wave," are distinctly unique and whose aetiology is similar to mankind. I believe that this group of angelic servers live for up to three thousand years on Earth. They have similar life experiences as we do e.g., they have a birth and death experience like us.

The '**Divine Blue Print**' is a sacred tool that we can use to access the 'Universal Life Force Energy' of the Angelic realms. Before we apply the principles of the Bagua, Trigram and Magic Square we are encouraged to take time out and embrace silence and solitude in our sacred oasis. Making a commitment to engage with the angelic realms and seek their instructions and guidance in our understanding of what the Bagua and Trigram means to us, will convey to our spirit a personal mandate from the Creator that will empower us to be co-creators of the Divine.

The secret messages that are contained within the 'divine blue print' will enfold as we take time to study and reflect on those messages imparted to us from the Divine Creator God/ess. Our garden designs will reap dividends when we are 'attuned' to spiritual values rather than guesswork.

The overall concept of the 'divine blue print' promotes a sense of destiny – our destiny. We are all 'light seekers' searching for a meaning and purpose to our lives. Listening and acting upon the sacred voices in our oasis will remove all of the 'negative forces' that separate us from the divine. There are times when, through human frailty, we are prone to moments of despair and bouts of loneliness. There have indeed been many occasions when I have succumbed to fear and its destructive influences. Coping with the adverse effects of prescribed medication as well as a depressive illness has taken its toll on my capacity to enjoy life. Fear needs to be dealt with speedily and swiftly if we are to win! In some uncanny way, fear reminds me of a hidden cancerous growth that needs the surgeon's scalpel for a complete, clear incision that will eradicate all evidence of further growth. Fear cripples our spirit and leaves us disempowered and disembowelled.

When we incorporate the principles of the 'divine blue print' and adapt our garden design to reflect these sacred influences we will experience a divine energy that saturates our very soul / spirit. The application of the specific colours as outlined in the 'angel circle' to our planting ideas will have a positive change in our ethereal connectedness with the Creator spirit as well as having a positive influence in our minds, hearts and relationships. Nothing can best prepare us for what can and will happen to our lives?

If we decide to create and angel peace garden incorporating the 9 squares under the specific influences of the named Archangels and work out the design according to the magic square we can expect positive 'chi,' divine angelic energy saturating our very being.

If you can remember the time when you first drove your car onto the highway or motorway, you had to take a series of lessons under the direction of an experienced car instructor, before you dare take life into your own hands. In other words, you placed your absolute trust in your driving instructor's experience and took to heart all their advice to help you pass your driving test first time! So it is when you work with angels and the Creator spirit. You have to learn the necessary skills that I call 'sacred tools.' These tools are so necessary if you wish to pursue your relationship with angels and the Creator.

Like falling in love with that all important date, it is important to know your partner as a valued friend before taking the 'bull by the horns.' Embracing love is about learning to love again but with different ground rules in place. The tools I am referring to are not gardening shears or a wheelbarrow. They refer specifically to prayer, meditation, silence, listening skills, contemplation, respect, simplicity, humility and reverence for everything that is connected with the 'divine.' I shall hopefully explain later, examples of what these are and how we can access the divine / angelic realms in our sacred angel peace garden.

Sean Bradley Academy of Therapeutic Channelling for Practitioners.

In Module 1*, we looked at the importance of the Celestial / Angel Bagua, can you briefly explain what this sacred tool represents and discuss whether it has a place in your therapeutic relationships with clients?*

The celestial angel Bagua represents the Four sacred energy areas North, South, East and West, and the four angelic forces /energy/ tone/colours /music, light and love and in the middle like an overlaying /light seal is the energy of Metatron / The Christ.

It is central to the technique as you invoke these energies. And as such you should tell your clients that you are going to call on the angels to assist. Janette F (Nov'04).

The celestial Angel Bagua means we are working with six important Angels, Metatron, Source, Michael, Gabriel, Raphael and Uriel –this leads us to be aware of our angels and our connection to them. They are there to heal us, to empower us and to lead us to become whole again, and when we can unconditionally love and forgive others, we can lead others to do the same, and bring them to their wholeness too. This is how we ultimately evolve and grow. **Suzanne B (Nov'04).**

The celestial Angel Bagua have inexhaustible sources of energy, knowledge and harmony which are at our disposal and this can and must be used during therapeutic /healing relationships with clients. The Bagua consists of the angels of Air, Water, Fire, Earth and the Elementals and divas and the 4 Spheres of Angels. Clients can be told how to contact this energy –e.g., by making a peace garden using the Angel Bagua as a blueprint. **Janet Q (Nov'04)**

The Bagua contains information, which can be referred to quickly and easily. It serves as a reminder as to where to invoke which Archangel and for each respective purpose, and helps when asking a client to visualize the colours during a treatment.

It can be adapted to many purposes e.g., when decorating a room placing sacred objects in the right place (a blue candle in the North for the Archangel Michael) to create a special place of peace and calm. **Paula .M (Feb '05.)**

The Sacred Tool of the Angel Healing Bagua is for using specific angels and therapeutic colour for healing specific parts of the body. For example, I would call on Michael, Archangel Prince of the North, the water Divas and the healing colour of blue if someone were having hearing problems (e.g. Tinitus). I would also call on each Archangel, angel helpers and healing colour as I pass my hands over that particular part of the client's body. Therefore, this is a very useful way of calling on the power of angels and focusing this power to specific parts of the body. **Martin T (Feb '05)**

THE ANGELIC HEALING BAQUA - this is the light, (color), sound, sensory, - vibrational RAY- by which the healing travels, via the Archangel Princes - who are Michael, Uriel, Gabriel, Raphael, and Metatron.

Depending on the different areas of the body, which require healing, and the various illnesses, which need treatment, -the appropriate specific Energy Area is used.

For Example: for problems with the ear. e.g. tinnitis - The Archangel Michael of the North, (who uses the color blue) is invoked .

THE HEALING TRIGRAM- Is the Divine Blueprint which soul - seekers and gardeners can use to create an Angel Peace Garden/ Sacred Space. i.e. plants or objects are used in the North, South, East and West in accordance with the particular color that is associated with the relevant Archangel. For example: Uriel of the East, is associated with the uplifting colures of yellow and orange.

INCENSE -this may be used to purify the atmosphere, before the Angelic Realm are invoked. The teaching explains the Law, shows how man's deviation from it is the cause of all his problems, and gives him the solution! ***Jeanne D.***

Supporting the Healing Process working with tree energies.

Stages of the Healing Process	Reaction	Relevant Tree	Beneficial Qualities
1. The Problem appears	I am shocked, hurt, knocked off balance, forced to re-evaluate.	Beech, Fir and Beech	Serenity, Confidence, Fluidity. Gentleness and reconciliation.
2. The ego resists.	I blame someone else or some external factor.	Hawthorne, Fir and Box	Alignment, Fluidity and Liberation.
3. Seeing what the problem reveals.	My mind finds a strategy to limit my suffering.	Broom, Walnut and Box.	Renewal, rebirth, Autonomy, Responsibility and Continuity and Liberation.
4. Experimenting with another attitude.	I identify behaviour that I could change, and try out a new attitude.	Fir, Hawthorne, Wild Rose and Pine.	Fluidity, Alignment, Openness, Light and Vitality.
5. New qualities come in.	The new behaviour has become part of me. I see the problem more objectively.	Pine and Walnut.	Light, Vitality, Autonomy and Responsibility.
6. The new attitude changes the situation.	The new situation gives me more inner freedom.	Box and Wild Rose.	Continuity, Openness and Liberation.
7. I integrate what has happened.	I am reborn, but need to take care that I do not slip back into old ways of behaving.	**Broom**	Renewal and re Birth.

Angels – Chakras in the Angel Peace Oasis

No's	1	2	3	4	5	6
Location	Root	Sacral	S/Plexus	Heart	Thymus	Throat
Colour	Red	Orange	Yellow	Green	A. Marine	Blue
Element	Earth	Water	Fire	Air	G.Angels	Air Realm
Kingdom	Mineral	Plants	Animal	Human	World/soul	Celestial

No's	7	8	9	10	11	12
Location	3rd Eye	Crown	Spirit	Spirit	Spirit	Spirit
Colour	Indigo	Violet	Silver	White	Gold/Wte.	Rainbow
Element	Archangels	Creator	Metatron	Thrones	Cherubim	Seraphim
Kingdom	A.Realms	A.Realms	A/Realms	Celestial	Celestial	Celestial

Chakra Chart associated with energy

Chakra	Colour	Energy Thoughts / Feelings.	Comments
1. Root	Ruby Red	Survival, sustenance concerns, such as money, shelter, and basic material needs	Anchors our physical body with energy. Develops during first (1-6) years of life.
2.Sacral	Orange	Physical and body issues and desires, appetites and addictions	Linked to a person's life (5-13 years) and creativity. The onset of puberty develops when Sacral chakra is fully developed/ matured.
3.Solar Plexus	Yellow	Power and Control	Linked to emotional development (13-19 years) adolescence period/ developed during teenage years.
4.Heart	Emerald Green with pink stripes	Love, Relationships, people attachments, forgiveness or unforgiveness.	Linked to the ability to have loving relationships.
5.Throat	Light Blue	Speaking truth and Communication	Linked to the ability to communicate and to express our creativity verbally.
6.3rd Eye	Dark Blue	The Future / the Past, Beliefs.	Linked to psychic ability and the Crown chakra.
7.Crown	Royal Purple	God, Religion, or Spirituality, Divine Guidance and Trust.	Linked to spiritual connection- God –Source and with the worlds around and the cosmos.

Kundalini: A personal pool of life force energy called Kundalini energy/ trickles out into our internal energy systems.

Kundalini flows more freely into each chakra when the chakras are fully developed. Kundalini flows up and out through the Crown chakra into the Universe.

We are all angels with but one wing,
And only by embracing each other can
we fly.

Anon.

To day, is the first day of the rest of your life.
Sean.

Section 4:

Therapeutic Channelling, working in partnership with the Divine.

- Therapeutic Channelling in a nutshell.
- Clues and fond memories of using touch
- Origins of Touch.
- History of Therapeutic Channelling
- Spiritual links in Divine Healing
- Article
- Personal notes on healing.
- Prayer to become a healer
- Pre assessment guidelines for clients accessing a treatment.
- A Channelled Treatment (academy version).
- Post treatment guidelines for client and therapist.
- A Christian perspective on supporting the healing process.

In a Nut Shell

I believe Therapeutic Channelling is:

Connecting with the Divine through touch.

It is a sacred tool that amplifies the healing process.

It empowers us to see God in our daily activities.

It empowers us to 'self-heal' all that is broken within us.

It releases angelic energies to assist us connect with our wounded inner child.

It empowers us to release all negative thought patterns, painful memories and anything that does not serve our 'highest good'.

Therapeutic Touch empowers us to reclaim the healing energies of the Lord Jesus and to see ourselves as a 'Child of God.'

The Divine energies assist us in working with the angelic realms

It is a sacred tool given to you by God.

Clues and Favourite Memories re: touch

There were many times when I was a young boy that the Local children would bring their sick pets for me to make well. I would say a prayer asking God and St Francis to heal them. Word soon got round and eventually my Granny had a word with me and asked me to stop turning her beautiful front garden into a hospital for sick animals. She was not too pleased but she was eventually won over and I have very fond memories of her helping me to make bandages out of old sheets. They were days of an innocent and childlike trust in God. My understanding of healing was somewhat childlike and it remains so to this day. Along the way some people have challenged my naivety and simplicity. I have always seen it as a strength rather that a weakness.

I recall an incident that occurred when I was five years old. My father was tidying up broken glass from the greenhouse and I being curious decided to go and investigate.

I fell into the broken glass. I still have the 'v' shaped scar on my leg. There was blood everywhere and my mum ran down the road to get my Granny. I believed that Granny had miraculous powers from God and I knew she would stop the pain and bleeding and make everything alright. She washed my leg and kissed it and I felt better instantly. It left a lasting impression on me. My destiny was set and some years later I went into healing work as a nursing monk.

In my childlike trust I believe that where there is love there is light and where there is light there is love. I believe that when we open our minds and ask God for help the help is given. I believe that the healing process begins as soon as we set our intention and desire to change.

In the late seventies and early eighties the nursing journals carried several articles on Therapeutic Touch and how nurses could enrol in specialist courses run by an American nurse called Kruger Kunz. It was a good course, which we all found beneficial but we all agreed that we had been using the energy already but had not given it a name. When I look back, I can see that channelling this energy was part of my daily routine.

It was not a conscious thing the energy had been flowing through me long before I realised it was there. The therapy that I offer to clients is not something that I invented it is a gift from God, another tool in the healing toolbox to use to help both others and myself. My hope is to empower them to heal themselves. I have many wonderful memories of the benefits of this healing which I have been privileged to administer.

On one occasion a good friend called round to see me, and after a few minutes I could tell from her body language that she was in a lot of discomfort. I gently held her hands and asked the angels to surround her with love. Then I invited Jesus to come and touch the areas which were causing her pain. There was no formal ritual or procedure; my actions were instinctive as I opened myself up to offer healing to this courageous soul.

In early 2003 I was booked to go and do an Angel Healing Day in a very nice hotel in Dublin. I was assured that it would be well attended and that I would more than cover my expenses. When I arrived at the conference room there were only two people waiting for me. My two sisters Eileen and Angela made the number up to four. The number four is significant is it the number of angel miracles. Miracles certainly happened for me that day.

One of the participants, Karen, told us of the years of child abuse she had suffered at the hands of her father. We were all very moved by her story and humbled by her openness. After we had done the healing process and meditation she shared that she had felt angels touch her and that she realised that she would have to deal with the abuse issue before she could move on. It was a good day, which all five of us enjoyed.

Later that night back at my sister Angela's house I was giving myself a hard time because of the low turn out. I was Also concerned because I had not made nearly enough money to even cover my expenses. I was doubting myself and questioning whether I should give up healing. My sister Eileen reassured me that the feedback from the day and all the previous workshops in Ireland was very positive and that I should keep going with the healing work.

On my return to the UK, I told the story to my dear friend Sister Agatha. She informed me "If I only touch one soul for God, then I had done the work of the Master." Those words have stayed with me ever since and I trust that all is as it should be regardless of the number of people in the room.

I met Karen again about four weeks later and she told me the rest of her story. The man who had abused her for all those years was actually her uncle and not her father. She discovered that her biological father was dying of cancer. He lived some distance away, but she felt she needed to go and make her peace, which she did. She said that the pure love she had received from the angels had empowered her to deal with it and then let it go. She hugged me and we shed many tears together.

In the summer of 2003 I was up a ten-foot ladder painting the outside of the house. I heard a 'thud' below me. When I looked down I could see a tiny creature lying on the ground.

I instinctively knew that something was badly wrong and my heart sank to the pit of my stomach. When I picked it up, I saw that it was a baby Blue Tit only a few weeks old.

There were no obvious signs of life and I felt sure that there was no hope for it. I cupped it in my hands and immediately invoked the angels of healing. I also sent out a plea to St. Francis to restore this tiny creature to life. After thirty minutes of cradling the bird, massaging its tiny frame and surrounding it with pure love and healing energy, there was at last a sign of life. The little bird suddenly stretched its wings and a few moments later flew back to the nest. That afternoon we saw quite a few of its relatives fluttering over and around our pond. We felt it was their way of saying thank you. Both the bird and I received a deep and meaningful demonstration of therapeutic touch that day and I truly feel that my prayers were most definitely answered.

When I first began to work with clients, I felt somewhat daunted by the thought of charging for the treatments, as at that time there seemed to be no formal structure to them. I had no formal qualification in it and at that time there were no books or courses on Therapeutic channelling available in my area. I prayed on it for some time and eventually I sensed that I was to be an 'open book' and to work from my heart centre and my intuition. This I did from a place of trust and I never looked back as they say.

The first few treatments I did on others went well and the clients assured me that they experienced something. They were not at that point too sure what it was, but they felt that it was very soothing, peaceful, and positive. Several of them have said they felt 'embraced by Jesus' while others have said they have seen Mary Magdalene kneeling beside me while I worked on their feet. This is not because I am more spiritual or highly evolved than anyone else, these beings make themselv es available to anyone who asks for, or offers healing with an open heart.

The use of oils in my work is not recent either. Throughout my nursing career I have always used oils to massage patient's hands and feet. When a patient in my care did not respond to conventional drug treatments or appeared anxious, restless or in pain, I would offer to massage their hands and feet.

They found the application of the oils to have a soothing and calming influence, which improved their overall comfort and general well-being. I also found that using massage with my terminally ill patients brought them comfort and eased their pain, helping them to sleep more peacefully.

My personal experiences and insecurities caused me to doubt the validity of my work at first. I felt like the 'new kid on the block.' It was such a totally different experience from my work as a nurse in which everything in my day was 'structured' and we had to work within clearly defined parameters. I was now working 'blind' and each treatment became and still is an act of faith. Before each treatment I would take time to prepare. I would sit in silent prayer for fifteen minutes or so asking that the client receive the highest level of healing possible.

All of my life I have accepted the communications I have received in trust.

Healing Notes –Active Participation.

Active participation includes asking a person what they are feeling, what they are seeing, where the pain is, how they would describe it and for any other details they can tell you.

Encourage client to actively take part and assume as much responsibility as possible during their healing session, even encourage them to direct the energy. Ask client to visualize the negative energy being pulled out and positive energy being put back in.

By frequently asking the client what they are feeling, seeing and sensing, you keep the client actively involved in the healing process. Keeping the client involved, they stay present with you and are aware of what is happening. The greater the active responsibility a person takes in their own healing process, the easier that process will be.

The more the client can feel their pain, describe the energy blockages and visualize the energy flowing, the easier it is to locate the blockages in the body and identify the challenge. Communication is vital if the treatment is to be successful in removing blockages and the input of energy.

One of the main benefits of this active participation is that the person is facing their illnesses / challenges head on. In doing this, they are confronting their fears and allowing the healer to support them, while both are working together to focus and direct the healing energy.

Including a person in their own healing process –by asking questions and having them describe what they are seeing, feeling, sensing – is one of the most powerful tools that a healer can employ. It will greatly enhance the results of the healing.

M Bradford " Hand's on Spiritual Healing."

Poem to the Butterfly.

Innocence
Black and Orange Butterfly –
Flying Joyously.

Wings like a nun's hands:
First folded in prayer,
They open in offering.

The Origins of Touch.

The auric manipulation and healing techniques that gave rise to Therapeutic Touch were derived from teachings found in Theosophy. Some study of charkas and Eastern energy systems will make the philosophy behind Therapeutic Touch more comprehensible, although it is not necessary to the practice. Like Western magical practitioners, Therapeutic Touch operates out of the experience that, ultimately all things in the Universe are connected. All exist as part of the Universal energy, which is why healers and patients alike can draw upon the Universal energy to supplement their own energy fields for healing.

A healer does not need to believe in this philosophy to be able to heal using Therapeutic Touch; s/he needs only the desire to help the patient. Nor does the patient need to believe in this philosophy: only be willing to accept help.

All human beings possess the healing ability that Therapeutic Touch trains; even children have been effectively taught to use it. Qualified Doctors and Nurses may have the advantage of knowing more specifics about functioning of the physical systems of the body, but they may also have the disadvantage of having to suspend disbelief in non-physical systems (such as energy fields) and their participation in disease. Lay people may not have the training in the psychology of the healer / patient relationship that Doctors and Nurses must have, but support groups offer both ongoing training and shared experiences and insight. Anyone with the desire and courage to heal can use Therapeutic Touch to make a real difference in many lives.

When I was training to become a State Registered Nurse (General) I was made aware of Therapeutic Touch through an interesting article in one of the American Nursing Journals. Therapeutic Touch was first developed in the early 1970's by an American Nurse, Dolores Krieger Ph.D. and her mentor Dora Kunz. The nursing profession throughout the world has encouraged nurses to adapt to the Principles and Practices of Therapeutic Touch in their nursing of clients. Today, in the UK there are recognised centres who subscribe to these beliefs and who encourage the Medical & Nursing Professions to incorporate Therapeutic Touch in there care delivery.

According to Dolores Krieger and her mentor, Dora Kung, Therapeutic Touch is based on the assumption that energy flows freely in and through the body of each healthy person. When illness strikes then this energy becomes blocked resulting in a downward spiral of negative emotions and illnesses that precipitate illness.

Therapeutic Touch is now being offered by nurses as well as qualified therapists to patients and their clients across the globe. It is a powerful therapy that really does benefit both client and therapist.

When we combine Therapeutic Touch with Therapeutic Channelling we become co creators of the Divine working in Partnership with the entire Angelic Realm.

The process of using Therapeutic Touch with Therapeutic Channelling (Energy and Spiritual Healing) is an acquired skill that involves specialist training for the therapist to proceed as a safe practitioner

As a Reiki Practitioner, I firmly believe in the concept of the 'Universal Life Force Energy,' that flows from the centre of the Universe (God). I believe that Universal Life Force Energy is 'Divine Energy' from the Creator flowing through my whole body right into my client.

The key to Therapeutic Touch

For potential therapists who desire to combine their therapeutic skills with therapeutic Christ /Angelic energies, channelling spiritual healing and restoring imbalance we devised a unique course that empowers you and I to work in closer partnerships with the Four Spheres of angelic servers, the Academy have been successful in developing a range of certificated courses from Beginner's to advanced level. See Section 6 for details about our range of courses for Practitioners covering all aspects of the process that describes the theory and practice of Therapeutic Channelling.

What is Therapeutic Channelling

Therapeutic Channelling is a sacred technique incorporating sacred oils and Therapeutic Touch working in partnership with the Angelic Realms. Angelic Channelling involves the Therapist connecting with the 4 Spheres of angels through using the 5th (Thymus) Chakra and the 8th (Crown) Chakras and by applying Therapeutic Touch to the two charkas spiritual healing begins.

Therapeutic Channelling is administered directly from the Angelic Realms, via the therapist to the client using both sacred oils to the client's feet, hands and to the nape of the neck. The process of administering sacred Therapeutic Channelling involves complete relaxation of the client for it to be therapeutic and healing.

There is no recorded evidence to support as to when Therapeutic Channelling first began. I believe that when the Creator created the solar system and the universe Angels were created primarily to glorify and praise their God. Then they were assigned the responsibility of administering 'healing light energy,' to everything that moved, that lived and breathed the Creator's breath. Another aspect of the angel's work is to supervise balance and restore imbalance within the created world of God's creation.

Therapeutic Touch

Therapeutic Touch is another recognised therapy that involves working with a person's 'energy fields' promoting relaxation of mind, body and spirit. The method of using Therapeutic Touch in this way has the desired effect of speeding up the 'healing process.'

The technique of applying Therapeutic Touch is usually performed without hands-on-contact by the Practitioner. Therapeutic Touch works with the interaction between the energy fields (auras) of the healer and patient. Physical contact is not necessary because at the level of physical proximity and focused intent used, the energy fields of the healer / therapist and patient are continuous. This is an active healing process; the healer must have an active intent for healing to occur, and the patient must desire (even unconsciously) a return to health. Therapeutic Touch can be practiced on babies, pets, plants as well as adults.

Research would now indicate that Therapeutic Touch does produce significant levels of effective healing. Clients and patients of mine have expressed an improvement in their sense of well being and respite from crippling pain and discomfort after a Therapeutic Touch session / treatment.

The key to practicing Therapeutic Touch is balancing a patient's energy. Pain or injury within the body or mind is reflected by changes in the energy field that surrounds and penetrates the physical body. With the healer's own energy field properly shielded and stabilized through meditation and centering, the patient's energy field is rebalanced, which will in turn allow the patient's own energy to effect the necessary healing. After the available energy is redistributed, the healer will often channel universal background energy into the patient's aura or energy fields as an extra reserve for the patient to use at will. Therapeutic Touch is a non-invasive practice that adheres to the ethical concerns about free will and doing no harm to the patient.

Each healer and each patient will interact differently; a healer must rely on his or her own intuition to decide how best to respond to whatever form a patient's energy takes. Imagery directs the healing; untangling knots of energy, warming cool areas, smoothing throbbing or rough spots or allowing a stream of energizing colour to flow through a patient's aura. Some healers will talk during a session, explaining continuously what they are doing or feeling. Some play meditative music and burn candles or incense. Many combine Therapeutic Touch with similar therapies such as hypnosis, massage or acupressure. Excessive energy can make a patient jittery or headachy.

Several Therapists who practice Therapeutic Touch use a model for healing that likens a living being's energy field to a cell membrane. It has pores or receptor sites through which the organism absorbs energy from its environment. I would consider it unethical to either block these sites or to force energy into or through them without the willing participation or permission of the patient / client. Sometimes, though, permission or conscious cooperation is impossible to obtain when a patient is in a comatose state; having a seizure; a baby, pet or plant......how then is healing to be effective. Basic survival instincts common to all living things generally act to maintain life, even when the organism is unconscious. I believe that it is perfectly ethical to send life energy to a being in need if it can be done in a way that does not compromise their free will. You can transfer life-giving energy through a smile, a friendly touch, an encouraging word or a focused thought.

As a senior nurse in Palliative care on night duty in the community, I regularly used Therapeutic Touch in these situations to deliver positive or even neutral energy to the outer edges of the energy field, where the patient or, and their partner / family members can accept and use the energy as it wills. Or not. Sometimes an organism may not want to heal. Perhaps it enjoys the attention it gets for being sick, or its spirit is just no longer up to dealing with a ruined body or an antagonistic world. That is a decision each being must make for itself. Healers (even well-intentioned ones) have no right to force the process, at least according to my spiritual beliefs.

A THERAPEUTIC TOUCH SESSION.

Therapeutic Touch is no miracle cure. Specific healing processes such as long bone repair and wound healing do appear to be accelerated by inclusion of Therapeutic Touch as a regular part of treatment. It is an adjunct or complementary therapy, however, meaning that it works with traditional Western medicine, not in place of it.

The main functions of Therapeutic Touch are:

- Relaxation.
- Pain Reduction.
- Regain a sense of calm.
- Balance one's energy fields (auras).

Achieving this helps the patient to take a more proactive as well as an active part in their own healing.

If the therapist is feeling unwell then a Therapeutic Touch session should be postponed until another day. Because I am using my own energy field as a conductor for the energy I will transfer into the patient's own energy field; if I am not balanced and confident of my ability to do this cleanly, I will be less effective for her.

Resume:

I think of Therapeutic Touch as serving many of the same functions in healing as a Navajo sing: helping the patient return to balance so that they can make best use of their own abilities to heal themselves. Even if complete physical recovery is not possible, the increased calm and reduction of pain help the patient meet the challenge of their illness or injury with confidence that they are not fighting it alone. They are connected; to the healer, to their environment, to the greater energy of the Universe. Therapeutic Touch presented in a context of Western medicine and thus has no specific spiritual orientation. But the spirituality behind the concepts used is undeniable. I have seen Buddhists, Native Americans, Theosophists, Aquarian New Agers, Wiccans, and Christians all successfully apply their own spiritual "spin" to their practice of Therapeutic Touch.

Christ has no body now on earth but yours

No hands but yours
No feet but yours
Yours are the eyes through which must look out Christ's compassion on the world
Yours are the hands with which he is to bless men now.
I am here only to be truly helpful
I am here to represent him who sent me
I do not have to worry about what to say or what to do,
Because he who sent me will direct me
I am content to be wherever he wishes,
Knowing he goes before me and with me
I will be healed as he teaches me to heal.
Krysia

Therapeutic Channelling challenges us to empower the spiritually impoverished in our society with 'the Christ Energies.'

As a Therapeutic Channeller 'working with the Christ energies,' we are reminded of our commitment to help those who are less fortunate, those who are in emotional turmoil, physical difficulty and financial strife. To love and assist the poor, however, is a risk that many of us do not think worth taking.

In a recent article in our Church bulletin I read the following extract; "As a child growing up, I thought that all the poor lived in Africa.

Images of the 1984 Ethiopian famine convinced me that poverty was a matter of food deprivation, easily remedied by donations to Band Aid, Cafod and Concern. Thus the poor were a far distant entity that others would fix if I contributed my penny's worth to the Lenten fast box. Even as a teenager, the poor always remained something 'out there,' people whom I never met who were afflicted by hardships that I did not understand. They were reachable through joining the St Vincent de Paul society or perhaps becoming a well-meaning nun.

Tired of hearing that I was meant to love the poor whilst having no poor visibly around me to love, I decided to do something about it. I'll go to Africa. That's where the poor are. Therefore I'll go and find some to 'do good' to. Six months were spent in preparation to join the missionary society as one of their lay associates. During that time, we spent one day a week doing pastoral work. I got to meet my first poor people: London's homeless at a Saturday soup kitchen. I was terrified.... what to say, how to relate, how to be friendly when they were not always the politest to us? So I stayed firmly behind the tea machine, dishing out the cuppas from a definite distance.

Having braved the initial shock of helping the homeless, I still wanted to go and love the African poor. Six months later I was on a plane to Nairobi, Kenya, to live and work with slum communities. I wanted poverty, and poverty is what I got. Slum houses of mud and stick, sewers running freely on the streets, AIDS and disease flowing from shack to shack.

No work, no food, no money. The job I got was with the poorest of them all. Little mentally and physically challenged kids, unable to sit, stand, walk or talk, many just staring at the ceiling hoping for someone to hold. We spent our days feeding, hugging, talking to these children who could often only respond with a glance of an eye.

And as time went on, these poor children revealed to us a different truth. For, though bound by barriers, they were free to love. They smiled and hugged without conditions, without us proving that we merit their affection. And as we discovered their freedom to love, we began to see our own poverty in loving one another. I began to see that, after all this time that I had been seeking out the poor to love and accept, it was I who was in fact poor and needing help.

It is hard to love the poor. It is hard to make the initial step towards the unknown, towards someone who has suffered what we cannot understand, towards someone who seems to us dirty or drunk or diseased. But once that step is made, our first fears can fade as real people emerge from behind the all-pervading problems. And with time, those whom we see as poor can slowly reveal to us our own poverty that we prefer to skilfully hide away. For when my poverty is seen by myself, I can choose to be healed and made whole again. So maybe reaching out to the poor, embracing the poverty within myself and within others could be a risk well worth taking."

When we embrace the poor we embrace the divine within our sacredness as well as within their divine being.

Regardless of who we are and what we have achieved in academic and material terms in our life, we are all equal in the eyes of our God/dess. Often, this truth is not as easy as it seems. We are all equal regardless of our position in society – our bank balance even our job. The poor man / beggar has equal rights to us as we jointly stand before the Divine Light.

Often we are challenged by our own 'agenda' to pretend to be somebody that we are not! Society does put enormous pressures on us to stop being ourselves and be somebody we are not! Today, lets face the all-important challenges that the Divine asks of us. Let us be our self and accept who we really are.

- That we are a child of the most High God/dess.
- That we are all 'co creators' of the divine.
- That we are unique and not a replica of another being.
- That our being is sacred.
- That we are joined to the divine lifeline.
- That our God holds us in high esteem.

- That we are chosen – Holy – divine- blessed.
- That we are ‘prophets of the most High God/dess.
- That our life matters here on Earth
- That we are here for a specific purpose.
- That we ask ourselves each and every day to be reminded that we are light workers empowered by the Christ Energies to touch the lives of those broken by man’s ignorance and pain.

We, on earth occupy a room on this earth.
And work is our rent for it.
HM Queen Elizabeth. Queen Mother.

Spiritual Links in Divine Healing

Creator God/dess

Archangels

Angels

Ascended Masters
(Holy men & women)

Spirit Guides & Loved Ones

You & Me

Clients

Global Village
(Community)

Creator

DIMENSIONS OF HEALING

Introduction:

1. The Spiritual Dimensions of Healing.

Working with the angels does not in any way eliminate the need for health care professionals. But it can facilitate the healing process on the subtle body, which is an important adjunct to the work you're doing in the physical world. We invite illness into our lives when we are out of touch with the negativity we are holding in our bodies, and when we don't know how to release it.

Ask your angel about the spiritual causes underlying the imbalance you are experiencing, and what you can do to facilitate their release. A condition can disappear or heal more rapidly once you have understood what is causing it. When you ask your angel for information about an illness, phrase your question in an open-ended way, for example: " What is it within me that needs to be healed?" Or "What are the lessons this illness is teaching me?" Don't ask, "Should I have chemotherapy or go on a juice fast?" Yes or no questions – questions involving critical choices – will usually be answered by your mind. And when you're sick, or addicted, the mind is riddled with fear.

For instance, this is what Leonard's angel told him when he asked what he needed to know about his gallstones: "Any anger held in the body will harden and block the flow. It is time for you to release your anger. It is time for you to release it with love toward yourself for having it, and with love toward the people you are angry at.

You know who they are. You don't have to tell them directly. Write them letters, and don't send them. Trust your angels to deliver the messages. And trust your doctor to do the rest. Also, you might try eating more green vegetables."

2. **HEALING WITH THE ANGELS.**

The more palpably you feel the presence of your angel, the stronger the conduit becomes for your angel to share its energy with you. When you are sad, tired, out of sorts, or feel the want of healing, sense your angel wrapping its wings around you. An angel hug can be a healing in itself. And you can work with you angel in other ways. Here's how I approach the scenario: " When I go to the doctor, I ask my angel to come with me. I feel its presence in the doctor's office, and I also sense my doctor's angel. Being aware of them retunes the situation and raises it to a higher frequency. This facilitates any kind of diagnosis and treatment.

"During my Reiki treatments I see and feel my angel floating above me, beaming golden light into the treatment points. It feels wonderful and deepens the release and healing."

3. **ALL THE HELP YOU CAN GET.**

When you are making a medical decision, use all the faculties that you have at your disposal, including input from your doctor, research on the condition that you or friends have done, information available from organisations or societies that work with that disease.

Use your celestial companions to help you clear and overcome fear so that you can make the choice of healing that suits you on all levels – physical, mental, emotional, and spiritual. The onset of illness and the recognition and acceptance of your addiction is the first step to healing. With your angel by your side, you can learn to welcome any and all manifestations as part of your healing. Calling on your personal guardian will also infuse you with the right attitude, one of compassion and understanding, of neutrality and acceptance. Calling on your angel opens you to love, which heals.

If a particular part of your body is in need of healing, invoke the presence of your companion angel. See and feel it beaming a healing golden light from the tips of its wings into the affected part. Invoke the healing angels, too, and see them surrounding your bed, bringing their love and support. You can also ask your angel for advice on how to work with this situation on the energy level. Again, this isn't to replace the work you do with a human healer. Rather, it adds to the effect by approaching the healing process from a spiritual perspective.

If you are undergoing any kind of medical procedure, rest assured that the room is filled with angels – yours, those of everyone there, and a flock of healing angels as well. Every time you are in need of healing, you open to the healer within you. You are not the victim of what needs to be healed – you are its student.

When you enter the classroom with your angels, you energise the opportunity to learn, and you magnify the wisdom that is coming to you.

The night before she was to have root-canal work, Valerie sat quietly and visualized her angel sending energy into her tooth. Then she took two aspirin and went to bed. During her previous visit, the dentist had examined her X ray and told her it was going to be a long and complicated procedure. But the next day, when he got into the tooth, the big problem he'd seen on the X ray simply wasn't there. He was able to complete the work in twenty minutes. The Dental Surgeon was perplexed. Valerie was grateful. When she got home, she lit a candle and sat quietly again, sending thanks from her heart to the angels.

Before undertaking a Reiki Treatment / Counselling session with clients, I always Reiki the room by using the power symbols to remove negative feelings and protect myself from attack by unwelcome spirits. Each new day, I always try to bless myself with the Reiki symbols and invoke the angels of the 4 spheres to protect me.

3. **ANGELS AND MEDICATIONS.**

Any kind of medication, vitamins, and minerals, herbal formulas that you are taking can be charged and aligned with your body by your angel. Hold whatever you are taking in your hands. Invoke your angel and see or imagine it touching the bottle or package with its wings. See its light energies pouring into the contents, energizing and tuning them to your body so there will be no side effects and they'll blend harmoniously with your body.

4. **HEALING (RX) LOVE**

If anyone you know is sick, visualize them surrounded by healing angels, glowing with a soft green-gold light. Healing isn't the same as curing. Healing means, " to be made whole" at every step of the way from birth to death. Sometimes it's through illness and in the midst of it that we become whole. Becoming whole again can happen in a variety of ways. And don't forget about the wiring angels. Sometimes what seems like an illness is a misdiagnosed case of rewiring.

5. **THE VISITING ANGELS' SERVICE**

When you visit someone who is ailing, invite the healing angels to accompany you. See and feel or sense them filling the room, and leave them there when you go. Remember that they can only come in when we invite them. If the person you are with is receptive to hearing about these heavenly healers, share what you know and how they have helped you. If not, it is more loving not to impose your experience, but you can always open your wings and fill the room with angel energy. This will benefit everyone who enters the room, doctors, nurses, pastors, counsellors, therapists, family, and friends.

Reflections on Life.

Many people will walk in and out of your life,
but only true friends will leave footprints in your heart.
To handle yourself, use your head; to handle others,
use your heart.

Anger is only one letter short of danger.
If someone betrays you once, it's his fault;
If he betrays you twice, it is your fault.

Great minds discuss ideas; average minds discuss events;
Small minds discuss people.

He who loses, looses much; he who looses a friend,
looses much more; he who looses faith, looses all.

Beautiful young people are accident of nature,
but beautiful old people are works of art.

Learn from the mistakes of others;
You can't live long enough to make them all yourself.
Eleanor Roosevelt

A Christian Therapist's perspective on:

God's Everlasting Comfort

When life becomes challenging, do you ever just want to run away from it?
To a place where no one knows you, and your problems are all erased?
You just want to find a hole, crawl into it, and hide....maybe forever?
Do you wish you were a child; again, depending upon someone else to take care of whatever life's challenges may come? Just to be held and told that everything is all right, and there is no need to worry?

In our Bible, Deuteronomy Ch:33 vs: 27 state, "The eternal God is thy refuge, and underneath are the everlasting arms." Whenever the challenges of life seem to be too much to handle – whenever you wonder what God was thinking when he laid a particular burden upon you, because surely you are not strong enough to bear it- God is there for you. God is there to hold you, in spirit. God guides you towards all solutions, all answers. God guides to you, all people, all resources, all sustenance that you need, each and every day.

We imagine, in our minds, that we let go, mentally, emotionally, and physically, all that worries us, all that causes us anxiety, and all that causes us fear.

As we imagine letting go, we can imagine God's everlasting arms holding us. Holding us closely and safely.

As we imagine being held by God, our breathing becomes easy and gentle. Our minds become calm and peaceful. Our bodies relax. Our emotions settle into Divine tranquillity.

As we rest, we are renewed by God's strength surging through us.

God's strength, God's intelligence, God's imagination are all ours to use within our lives. As we let go, we let God work and play through us, bringing us through our challenges. Bringing us to God's absolute peace.

Throughout the day, we are reminded that God is with us, guiding us through each and every decision. We can depend upon God to guide us, effortlessly, safely, and loving. God tells us that everything is all right; there is no need to worry.

What is now expected of you as a qualified Therapeutic Channeller is that you are invited to:

- Nurture each other and all the members in your group and in Therapeutic Pathways Consultancy across the global village through regular contact.
- Try to attend regular group meetings and nurture the 'core values' of the Foundation.
- Help spread the word about Therapeutic Channelling through 'word of mouth..' This is by far the best way of dealing with fear and ignorance surrounding our work on behalf of the angels.
- On the First Anniversary of your qualification, you are encouraged to do a 2 day retreat and spend time alone reflecting on your life's work and sacred gifting as a Channeller of Divine Healing /angelic energies.
- You are invited to become a registered qualified trainer by undertaking our in-house courses in

  1) The Teaching & Practice Certificate Course.
  2) The Master's Certificate Retreat Residential Course.
  3) The Advanced Master's certificate (Due Spring 2005).

Therapeutic Channelling "Working in Partnership with Angels to Heal-Restore & Balance Lost-Energy."

Therapeutic Channelling is a unique sacred therapy that precedes all modern day therapies as it dates back to when the Creator crated man and woman in the 'divine likeness of God.'

Throughout history mankind has practised some form or another of 'therapeutic touch.' In ancient Roman and Egyptian cultures as well as certain religious traditions, great emphasis was placed on welcoming one's fellow guests by washing their feet. In the Jewish and Christian traditions there are many recorded examples in the Old Testament of the Prophets initiating the sacred traditions of washing and anointing another's feet.

Therapeutic Channelling touches our very souls when the Divine God/dess transfers spiritual healing from Spirit through Spirit in Spirit for Spirit with Spirit to Spirit. The divine healing energy is administered to us through the gift of 'Therapeutic Touch.' We are empowered to reclaim our 'First Love' and 'Our Lost Child Within,' working in 'Partnership with the Angelic realms.'

I believe that the Creator God/dess touches us indirectly and directly. I also believe that when the Creator created the 4 Spheres of Angelic Servers it seemed right that they would also be used to '**channell'** the Creator's divine healing love & the 'Christ energies' to you and me.

When we experience **Therapeutic Touch** we experience the presence of our God/dess in our lives at a deeper and richer level than ever before. In our 'spiritual poverty' our divinity become enriched.

Therapeutic Channelling involves working with the 'Angelic Realms' through the healing properties of 'therapeutic touch' empowering us to reclaim the lost child within our being and experience for the very first time the presence of our 'First Love.' This first love is God's unconditional, selfless, respectful and reverent healing love for you and me. It is our free gift from our God/dess by divine birthright.

When we open our lives to this sacred energy we become infused with divine love that transforms our human weakness. The angels who are present before we begin the treatment empower the therapist to work in partnership with them in the recycling of our negative energies into a positive healing energy. In turn, there is a positive cumulative desired effect that re-energises our soul and our spirit, enhancing our awakening to the divine in and around our sacred space.

Therapeutic Touch is about connecting to another's life force spirit working with the 'Christ Energies' & 4 Spheres of Angels through the sacred symbols of oils, gentle massage and touch.

When we invite the angelic realms to join us in the therapy we receive ethereal energy that encapsulates all negative energies restoring balance and 'chi' energy. Lives are completely restored on a physical, spiritual and mental level. The results are indeed overwhelming. In our humanity, we underestimate the power of therapeutic touch in our daily lives.

A modern phrase 'seeing is believing,' does challenge each one of us to take the penultimate step or leap of faith to experience the inner sacredness and divine healing properties that are associated with **Therapeutic Channelling**. One does not have to be a Christian or a believer to receive therapeutic channelling! All that is asked of us is that we humbly, sincerely and reverently respect the energies imparted to our being.

We have brought together a unique course in Therapeutic Channelling covering **5 Modules over 6 days**. The course will empower you to work in Partnership with the Creator God/dess and with the 4 Spheres of Angels as a certified Channeller. For details of our forthcoming courses, venues & costs please see section 6 in the book.

CONFIDENTIAL

Client Treatment Assessment Files

Name	
Address:	
Tel: No's:	
e-mail address:	
Other:	

Interview Checklist

Initial Reason for visit:	
Current Medical Problems:	
Any H/O Mental Illness etc:	
Medication:	

Treatment Checklist: Energy Problems

Discuss actual Treatment:	
Scan Chakras and Aura	
Having identified problem -Relax client - Use appropriate colour for meditation visualization, release and cleansing of charkas.	
Closure and Grounding exercise	
Discuss further visits and agree appointment date:	

Assessment / Feedback of Treatment........

Therapeutic Channelling Treatment.

'Working with the Christ / Angelic energies to Heal, Restore & Balance Lost-Energies.'

The therapeutic treatment usually last for 60 minutes and consists of:

- Brief introduction to the therapy session (5 mins).
- Take a brief summary of client's details (name, tel number, etc/ 5 mins).
- Sit client in the upright position, or a position most acceptable for the client, and assist them to relax and feel comfortable and safe.
- In silence, place both of your hands on the client's head (The Crown Chakra) and quietly invoke the 4 Archangel Princes (Michael, Gabriel, Raphael and Uriel). Continue to hold both hands in this position for at least 5 - 8 mins.
- Position yourself facing the right side of your client. Gently place your left hand on the client's head and at the same time place your right hand between the throat and heart areas of the client (The Thymus Chakra). Again invite, Invoke and Ask the 4 Archangel Princes together with all Four Spheres of Angelic Servers to come and assist you now in this treatment. Continue to keep both hands in situ for at least 10 mins.
- Following this sacred attunement exercise, ask your client to remove their shoes, tights / socks etc. I would recommend that you encourage your client to choose the position best comfortable for them. i.e. either lay your client down on a treatment couch, or sit in a comfortable chair with both feet and legs supported on a footrest. Place a soft towel under their feet and lower legs and keep your clients warm and free from any draughts.
- Quietly and gently encourage your clients to relax and observe the rhythm of their breathing. Play soft relaxing music to soothe their anxious / worried thoughts.
- Ask you client to visualize resting in a safe place. Working from the client's head down to the tips of their toes, encourage the client to focus on the pockets of negative energy being pulled down from the very top of their head and out of their body by the

angels of healing through the gentle strokes / massage techniques now being used.

- Apply sacred oils to your hands and using gentle downward / upward strokes massaging the clients lower legs down to the tips of their toes. Use a visualization of the angel's bringing the client's 'negative energy' down through the tips of their toes and to visualize the angels taking this negative energy from their body into their sacred healing baskets. Continue to use this technique for at least 10 mins on each foot / leg.
- Then administer sacred oils to both legs encouraging the client to visualize the healing angels bringing their restored, transformed negative energy now Positive energy back into their body via their head; down their neck, shoulders, arms, hands. The positive energy is being poured down through the upper chest, around all of the organs and down into the abdominal region and down through the pelvic area into the upper and lower limbs into the feet. Continue to do this for a further 10 mins.
- Continue to relax and reassure your client.
- With the client's permission, ask them to place both hands on a towel situated above their abdominal area (stomach).
- Taking one hand at a time, place some of the sacred oil and massage the oils gently into their hands and wrists. This should take only 5 mins per hand. Encourage the client to relax and experience the gentle healing touch of their God through the angels right now. Reassure the client that this process is to acknowledge their divine angelic nature and unique gifting as a co creator of the Divine.
- Immediately following the anointing of the hands, position yourself in the upright position and stand on either the left or right side of the client, whichever is the most comfortable for you. Facing the client, place both hands on their Crown Chakra and invoke the Christ energies and the energies of the Archangel Princes to join you now in the forthcoming powerful healing exercise that will bring closure to the treatment.
- **First in breath** – now verbally invite the Archangel Michael (Archangel Prince of the North) invite the client to relax. In their first in breath, invite the client to now visualise the colour blue

(Michael) coming down through their Crown Chakra, and invite the client to sense the healing vibrational colour and essence of blue as it enters the Heart Centre. In they're out breath; invite the client to send out love and healing light to the world.

- **Second in breath** – now verbally invite the Archangel Uriel (Archangel Prince of the East) invite the client to relax. In their second in breath, invite the client to now visualise the colour Yellow / Gold (Uriel) coming down through their Crown Chakra, and invite the client to sense the healing vibrational colour and essence of Yellow Gold as it enters the Heart Centre. In they're out breath; invite the client to send out love and healing light to the world.
- **Third in breath** – now verbally invite the Archangel Gabriel (Archangel Prince of the South) invite the client to relax. In their third in breath, invite the client to now visualise the colour Jade Green, streaked with pink, (Gabriel) coming down through their Crown Chakra, and invite the client to sense the healing vibrational colour and essence of Jade Green with streaks of pink as it enters the Heart Centre. In they're out breath; invite the client to send out love and healing light to the world.
- **Fourth in breath** – now verbally invite the Archangel Raphael (Archangel Prince of the West) invite the client to relax. In their fourth in breath, invite the client to now visualise the colour Pink, Red and Crimson (Raphael) coming down through their Crown Chakra, and invite the client to sense the healing vibrational colour and essence of Pink, Red and Crimson as it enters the Heart Centre. In they're out breath; invite the client to send out love and healing light to the world.
- **Finally** – now verbally invite the Angels of the Violet Flame (Representing Christ Consciousness) invite the client to relax. In their final in breath, invite the client to now visualise the colours of the Violet Ray coming down through their Crown Chakra, past their Throat Chakra. Now invite the client to sense the healing vibrational essence of the Violet Rays (The Christ) as it enters their Heart Centre. In they're out breath; invite the client to send out love and healing light to the world.

- To conclude –invite the client to visualise the White light of Divine Love coming from the Heavens down into their Crown Chakra, saturating their mind –their entire body –every organ, tissue and muscle with the pure white light of God's love for them as a Child of God.
- Now invite the client to invite and ask the Archangel Michael to come and put a seal on their Crown Chakra preventing any escape of healing energy from their body and higher self. Invite to client to call upon Michael to place them in a Pyramid of the purest white light and protect them from all negative mindsets.
- At this point, finally scan the client's aura and place a seal of Divine Love and Light over the client, running both your hands down from the client's head, right down their arms and body.
- Using the Client Information Post Treatment Fact Sheet Leaflet, read the positive affirmations to the client and invite them to repeat each affirmation after you –thus reprogramming the client's DNA from a negative to a positive mindset. Invite the client to say the Affirmations 3 times daily as per information leaflet for 30 days.
- Assist your client to feel relaxed and when they feel ready to open their eyes and connect to their immediate surroundings assist them to put on their shoes.
- It is strongly recommended that the client should be encouraged to rest for a short period after this treatment before driving a car, etc.
- The client should be encouraged to drink plenty of water following angelic therapeutic channelling as the treatment releases harmful toxins (free radicals) that need to be flushed from the client's body and ethereal energy field.

Client's Information "Post Treatment Guidelines"

RECOMMENDATIONS FOR THE CLIENT

- **I suggest that you invite the client to reflect, in a period of silence, on what has happened. Suggest a walk before driving home.**
- **Remind the client that the way forward is to connect and work from the 'Heart Centre' and avoid going to the Head Centre!**
- **Before the client leaves you, assure them that in the event of anything unforeseen, that they can contact you. Encourage them to phone you in office hours), unless it is an emergency.**

Behold
Enfold
Embrace
Enjoy
The
Presence
Of
God
And
The
Healing
Touch
Of
Angelic
Divine
Energy.

Spiritual Workout

To maintain your inner peace and presence of mind may I suggest that you do the following:

- Create a special place (Prayer Corner) with some fresh flowers and there light a candle and burn some incense where you can engage with the Angelic Realms.
- Decide what time is best for you and make time to enjoy time spent in meditation.
- Wear loose fitting clothes.
- Ensure room is warm, comfortable and safe.
- Focus on the rhythm of your breathing.
- Following a treatment, may I recommend that you drink plenty of water (2 pints) will remove all harmful toxins that have been released during the healing session.
- If you are feeling tired and exhausted, may I suggest that you take a restful break?
- When taking a shower, invite the Angels of the Water Realm to wash, cleanse and balance your Aura and Chakras –visualize all negative thought patterns and any impurities being washed down the plug hole –then seal it with the heel of your foot.
- You may like to purchase one of our products, i.e. a Healing/relaxation CD, E-Books, or visit our Website Links Page www.sean-bradley.com for angel statues, incense, etc.

Following a treatment, you may experience a lethargy, or a sense a major shift or experience a sense of inner peace.

If you need advice and support, please feel free to make contact with your therapist.

In the event that you are unable to travel to see your therapist, you should be able to discuss your concerns with one of our team over the telephone.

Should you require longer, then we may have to look at other options, i.e. a follow-up session / possibly a full day on a residential /non-residential consultation.

ITINARY FOR TREATMENTS:

Non-Residential 1 day Consultation: Arrive before 10 am –Depart 4pm (6 hours) Consists of 2 in depth '1 to 1 sessions' including channelled healing using oils, incense and discovering your 'Named Archangel at Birth. Lunch & refreshments included.

RESIDENTIAL 1 Night/ Day Consultations. (Full Board and materials included). Clients can choose one of two treatment plans. Plan A (18 hours) or Plan B (24 hrs). Clients are invited to arrive around 6pm in time for the evening meal.

The overall aim is to nurture an environment that is conducive to working with strong powerful negative, positive, physical, mental and spiritual emotions that demand a place of sensitivity, feelings of safety, peace, honesty and professional integrity.

You can now book Online -Please visit website for further details and Booking forms. **www.sean-bradley.com**

Your Daily Prayer

Holy Father /Mother God, I ask for the outpouring of Holy Spirit, together with the support from the Lord Jesus, Mother Mary, St Francis, the Archangels Michael, Gabriel, Uriel, Raphael, Metatron; all the Archangels, Healing angels, my Guardian Angel and all Guides, Nature Beings who work for the Divine Light, to now assist, cleanse me of all negative thought patterns, impurities and strengthen me, my loved ones and all those who have helped me reclaim my inner child.

I now invite, invoke and ask that I be blessed by God and prepared as a Channel of Divine Healing Love for all who now seek my help.

I ask that you bless my being; these humble hands and that you accept all that I am in service of these sacred healing energies.

As a Child of God, I thank you for your love today.

Daily Affirmations

(Say each morning-noon and last thing at night –3 times daily for 30 days)

- I am getting better and better every day, in every way.
- I am a whole and perfect Child of God.
- I am perfect just the way I am and I choose to continue to grow and evolve into my full potential.
- Spirit goes before me, making my way easy, harmonious and successful.

FORGIVENESS AFFIRMATIONS

- I, (insert your name) now forgive myself for all the pain and suffering I have caused myself on all levels in all ways since the beginning of time.
- I forgive myself right now.
- I, (insert your name) am now willing to release the need for (list problem) in my life. I (insert your name) release it now, accepting and trusting God, Holy Spirit and the Angelic energies and the process of life to assist me to heal and to meet all my needs and desires in a healthy way.

BEHOLD -ENFOLD -HOLD -LISTEN
TO YOUR HEART CENTRE -YOUR TEACHER

PRAYER OF PROTECTION TO ST MICHAEL

Holy Michael, Archangel,
Defend us in the day of battle;
Be our safeguard against the wickedness and snares of the evil one.
May God rebuke Satan, we humbly pray:
And do thou, prince of the heavenly host,
By the power of God, thrust down to hell Satan,
And all wicked spirits who wander through the world
For the ruin of souls.
AMEN

Prayer to the Holy Spirit of Source

Father, pour out your Spirit
upon your people,
And grant us a new vision of your power,
A new faithfulness to your Word,
And a new consecration to your service,
That your love may grow among us,
And your Kingdom come:
Through Christ our Lord.
AMEN

The Onion

By Sr Agatha

If we contemplate the onion it can reveal so much of God to us. The Onion is, "**ME**".

The corpus of the onion is an analogy of my pilgrimage to God. The onion consists of many- many layers –these can be regarded as layers of life experiences that we have accumulated including our weakness and negativism, our passions.

The path of holy poverty calls us to surrender all to God. There comes a time when we must allow God to unwrap us so that we may become more totally His. When unwrapping the onion some layers will come away from the corpus of the onion more easily, others will cling to the corpus of the onion. When we peel the onion as we approach its heart if we then planted its heart it would spring to life, none of the discarded wrappings would bring forth life.

When the onion is unwrapped it brings forth tears- but the tears cleanse. If we followed the unwrapping of the onion by Our Heavenly Father to its conclusion, opening the final layer we are left, humanely speaking, with nothing, but from Gods perspective the naked soul stands before him waiting for his embrace.

You may say that the onion smells, life in the raw is often squalid, the stench of sin /wickedness, but we can learn to look beyond the aroma, beyond the tears to Him.

As we journey through our faith journey (Lent) let us figuratively speaking unwrap the onion layer by layer, surrendering to God that which we know hinders us upon our journey. The onion has a dried stalk almost like the umbilical cord; we are all children in the great womb of God.

Do Not Judge.

We should not judge by external appearances and we should accept that we do not know the whole picture in any given situation. If an onion were placed before a statue in church a reaction could be, "shocking", disgraceful, cracked exhibitionist…but you and I know that the onion has been illuminated by the Holy Spirit of God becoming a sacramental that was teaching us something about God.

Onions need to stretch out to Gods world and absorb whatever is good, sunlight, air a degree of moisture, then they will grow. If an onion is too introspective it will find only tears. Go out and meet the presence of God. Onions are all individuals, cut an onion in half, paint on the surface and then print on a piece of paper, the imprint will be unique to the specific onion, so is the imprint that we make on the life of others....we are irreplaceable and we are loved by God as we are.

To each of us the onion will say something different, what will it say to you?? The Onion.

THE GREAT INVOCATION

From the point of Light within the mind of God

Let the light stream forth into the minds of men

Let the Light descend on Earth

From the point of Love within the Heart of God

Let love stream forth into the hearts of men

The purpose guide the little wills of men –

The purpose, which the Masters know and serve.

From the centre which we call the race of men

Let the Plan of Love and Light work out

And know that the door is sealed where evil dwells.

Let the Light and Love and Power restore the Plan on Earth.
Djwhal Khul

God is served only when He is served according to His will.

St Pio of Pietrecina

Section 5:

Anecdotal evidence supporting Therapeutic Channelling

- A Reflection –When heaven touches us
- A Case study –client
- Feedback from our student therapists.
- Feedback from our from clients, qualified therapists and our student therapists.
- Reflection

When Angels Touch Us Heaven moves closer towards us!

The Spirit of the Lord
Has been given to me for
He has anointed me
He has sent me to bring
The good news to the poor,
To heal the broken hearted,
Give sight to the blind, and freedom to the
Downtrodden.
Luke 4: 18

Therapeutic Channelling, as a Healing Therapy.

Similar to an Eastern traditional healing therapy called Reiki, this method relies on channelling through the Christ Energies via the Angelic Realm and pivots on information, which was given to Moses, when he received the Ten Commandments. The general consensus is that Moses did not feel that everyone was ready to receive this information, so it was given to the few faithful, who practiced the teachings. The Teachings of the Essenes can boast to being a BLUE-PRINT for solving the problems of the individual - and thus, ultimately, - WORLD PROBLEMS!

The Therapy, which derives from it - owes much of its increasing popularity today, to ex- monk, Sean Bradley, who teaches therapists form his Academy in Storth, Cumbria.

THE AIMS OF THE COURSE:

These are to: provide an easily accessible vehicle, by which interesting and useful information can be delivered to like -minded people, who would also subsequently be able to access the Beginner's course and ultimately go on to be Practitioners in Therapeutic Channelling.

THE CONTEXT IN TODAY'S SOCIETY

The pressures of modern day life are causing more and more stress – related and psychosomatic illnesses, and in a growing disillusionment with western medicine and with the availability of more leisure time, in a worldwide quest-more and more people are looking for 'food for the soul' and a way to bring back peace and harmony into their lives.

Thus the popularity of Alternative and Complementary Therapies is growing to the extent, that even the once suspicious orthodox medical profession, are taking a more holistic approach and referring patients for treatments such as Aromatherapy etc.

Patients themselves are taking matters into their own hands, in trying some of the Eastern Therapies, such as Reiki healing which have been around for some 2000 yrs.!

This is in comparison to our Western Orthodox Medicine, which can only boast several centuries!

THERAPEUTIC CHANNELLING

Is another such therapy, which is really gaining momentum and was practiced by the Essenes up to 8ooo yrs ago and around the time of Jesus Christ?

As mentioned, the therapy relies on ***ANGEL POWER***.. Although there are some 385 direct references in the Bible, Orthodox Religions have sadly neglected angels.

Perhaps this is because by using Angels to intervene for us at the throne of God, (although we don't need to do that, as we have a direct link) we are in less need of the clergy, as it puts the power back into the hands of the individual!

Angels seem to enjoy an increase in popularity every 20 years or so, but many people appear to have forgotten their credibility. They appear to overlook the fact that it was angels who heralded the birth of the Christ-child, and all the other references to them which are in the Bible and books of other major world religions, such as Islam, Maori, Shinto and Hindu.

In fact, Angels, since the beginning of creation are celebrated throughout mythology, and angelic visitations at a more personal level, along with delivery from adversity, are becoming more and more discussed.

As is borne out by the fact that, in a recent survey, it was found that many people can name at least three Archangels-these being Michael, Gabriel and Raphael

IN CONCLUSION

This Therapy is compatible with almost all of world religions, and does not rely on Christianity. The Divine Energy and angels existed before the birth of Christ.

(Christians believe in the Holy Trinity - comprised of The Father, the Son and the Holy Spirit). The Energy remains unchanged.

The Divine Energy and angels exist -unreliant of a belief in their existence.

In fact, more and more of the scientific community are coming back to the proposition that in the face of such a creation as the universe/ multiverse -- there MUST exist a Creator. On many fronts in the scientific fields, there are steps nearer to the proof of this. It is only a matter of TIME before proof is conclusive.

Who knows what exists between the molecules of a piece of wood-which was previously thought to be solid!!!

The Teachings of the Essenes provide a Divine Blueprint for a Therapy which speaks to the Human Condition and can **CHANGE LIVES** by teaching Man that by deviating from God's LAW, he is the cause of his own destruction, and that of his own Planet- (as described by our Scientific Experts).

Just by communing with the Angels and Nature Realm as God intended at the Creation, and by transmuting all negativity into Love, Man can HEAL himself, (as sons and daughters of the Creator) and his planet, and in doing so SOLVE WORLD PROBLEMS!

Sean Bradley has specially designed this course, to help to Facilitate this, in reliance on the preceding information.

May the Angels of Light and Love dwell with anyone reading these words. Jeanne Drinkel TCCP CTSBA

THE METHOD OF THERAPEUTIC CHANNELLING

WHEN CHANNELLING-

The sitter is encouraged to relax, and possibly engage in a short meditation, to 'tune in ' to the Angelic Realm, the Archangel Princes Michael, Uriel, Gabriel, Raphael, Metatron, and the Angel Source are INVITED, INVOKED to bring through the Christ Energies, and THANKED for their Presence.

The hands may be placed on the sitter's head or shoulders or even just the aura, the sitter's feet may be anointed with sacred oils during the treatment.

THE BENEFITS OF THERAPEUTIC CHANNELLING

Angels are a very powerful force who is only too keen to help and love us unconditionally, and all we have to do is ask!!

Jesus himself said ***"ASK AND IT SHALL BE GIVEN UNTO YOU"*** Just be as specific as possible what is asked for!

As a Therapy, the rays are channelled through from the highest realms, it is a very beautiful, healing and uplifting experience.

An indescribable feeling of peace and tranquility may descend on both channeller and sitter, along with beautiful white and golden light, (in accordance with anecdotal evidence.)

What exactly happens during the treatment is very hard to describe, but usually, both channeller and sitter report that something extra-ordinary occurs.

The therapy speaks to the human condition and can **CHANGE LIVES** - by:

Empowering the sitter to change negative mind sets, enlisting the help and guidance of the angelic realm in everyday matters, self-healing mind, body and spirit, restoring balance and reducing stress, promoting well - being and even lengthening the life-span of the believer who puts the Teachings into practice.

The therapy can be used on anyone who wishes to achieve any of the above benefits, and is completely ***SAFE.***

SACRED TOOLS

These may be used to help facilitate the use of the therapy, and may include:

FAITH-

It is sometimes difficult to take on board which we cannot see, however-take a leap of faith, and know that your angels will be there to answer you. The answer may not be the one you wish to hear, but it will be for your highest good.

SILENCE-

This has been described as the ***"Sister of the Divine"*** It is in the silence that the 'still small voice' may be heard! We do not always get an answer straight away, but you will be answered!

SACRED OILS-

These are oils, which have been blessed by the Angelic Realm, and may be used to anoint the feet or head of the sitter.

A Case study

As a Reiki Teaching Master and Holistic Therapist I had worked with the healing energies of the Angels for a number of years. I had invoked the energies of specific Angels for whatever my needs or the needs of others were and received immediate results. For instance, Archangel Michael for safe travelling, I would ask for Michael's strength, focus and protection and His "Armour of Steel" would wrap itself around the person or persons in need with immediate. However, when I was struck down with a very nasty Pneumococcyl Pneumonia at the end of April 2002, I was not able to help myself as it absolutely stopped me in my tracks. This led to Chronic Fatigue and other complications.

It was at this time that two very good friends were able to have the pleasure of meeting Sean at an Oldham Health Fair in December 2001. Prior to my illness, I had been given details of this event with a view to having a stand myself but declined the offer as I had a successful business and was working to capacity alone with a very hectic family life which filled my days completely. In the meantime, I had fallen ill and as I had passed details onto others, I was to become very thankful that two good friends, were able to attend. Both friends telephoned me to tell me that they had met this wonderful man who worked with Angels and that he had the most wonderful healing hug. I started to feel so much better in the days following. I felt a sudden lifting of my symptoms and did not realise at the time that my friends, who were concerned with my health, had explained my predicament to Sean, who in turn had been sending me healing. Up to that time, I had really struggled hard and couldn't accept help from others.

Karen felt strongly that she should somehow get me to see Sean who at the time lived in North Manchester. In fact the day a group of us landed on his doorstep all his worldly goods were in packing cases ready for his forthcoming move to Cumbria. On meeting Sean I felt immediately encompassed in his heart (and slippers) and had the most uplifting experience. The four of us received '1 to 1' treatments and even prior to my '1 to 1' the beautiful calming voice and energy was to reduce me to uncontrollable tears.

Just hearing Sean's voice allowed the tears of release to quietly fall whilst his wonderful words wafted over us. When it was my turn to have my "experience," I just gave myself up to the healing energies. As I sat in a chair alone with Sean, he brought in the Archangel Princes and all the Angels, and immediately I was taken on a wonderful journey. As Sean worked with the Angels, I had the feeling that my arms were being taken up sideways to the level of my shoulders. After trying to fathom out I realised my physical arms were still by my side with my hands on my lap and Spiritually my arms had been lifted up. I just gave myself up to the most wonderful healing experience I had ever received. I was mentally taken to another place and when I had worked it out why I was lifted up and who those people were on the ground, the tears were unstoppable. I had been given the ultimate shared experience of our Lord Jesus on the Cross. Sean was then to anoint and massage my feet and he was Mary Magdalene. The realisation was incredible and so unexpected and so awesome. After the treatment, I was very unsteady and dizzy.

The whole experience had a profound spiritual impact on my soul. I had never, ever experienced this before. Immediately after my treatment, Sean invited me to rest on one of the spare beds, as I needed time to myself and to come round and come back to reality. Eventually, the relief after all the months of illness was immense and gave me a great kick start.

A week later, my friend and I visited Sean for another 1 to 1 treatment. I felt strongly that my friend needed this same experience and amazingly I insisted on driving. What was so amazing was that I hadn't been able to drive for months. I had recovered the strength and mental alertness to not only take the lead role but to <u>actually drive!</u> On this occasion, I received a 'top up' and was to have the utter pleasure of hearing Sean's Angelic Singing Voice. The tears inevitably flowed and I was again to experience the beautiful healing and unconditional love of Sean.

After Sean settled into his new home in Cumbria, it was soon opened up as a Healing Sanctuary. On Good Friday 2003, a group of us travelled to Cumbria for the most wonderful Retreat Day, which was to bring about such a change to my life and also the lives of my family. We experienced not only Sean's group Angel Healing, where again I was to experience the emotions of our Lord Jesus on the Cross. Time was also spent in Sean's wonderful Angel Healing Peace Garden. As we listened to the magical sounds of clearing and cleansing running water and the summer breeze playing with the wind chimes a visualisation came to me. My husband and I were cycling up to Sean's lane and I absolutely **knew** we were to come to live there soon! Well I didn't know how it was going to happen but I couldn't wait to tell Sean and my friends that I was going to be Sean's neighbour!

And yes, it just happened quite magically that …..Months later, we were moving into a lovely bungalow just yards down the lane from Sean. This was to be our retreat, our bolthole and three months later, I can look back with the realisation that Sean's healing energy has had a knock-on effect on my whole family. We have so far enjoyed such wonderful long weekends, family and friends celebrations and many more to come.

Thanks to my two friends' meeting with Sean, I am not only on the road to recovery but my husband and I have a much better quality of life altogether. Thank you Sean from the bottom of my heart. **Coleen - Manchester**

Feedback from our student therapists.

Dear Sean, I can only describe what it means for me to experience therapeutic touch/channelling, as it will be a different experience for each individual. For myself it is;

- Sensing angelic energy pulsing through my body from head to toe
- Being still and calm in the presence of the angelic realm and God
- An inner peace
- Release of emotional blocks
- Healing touch (foot wash)
- Being emotionally touched

Benefits will depend on the individual experience and their level of enlightenment (openness). For myself, the benefits are soothing, comforting, and humbling. It is allowing myself to 'be touched' in ways that I don't necessarily expect, trusting with faith that God and the angelic realm are working to heal me in preparation to do Gods will. I do not as yet have a sense of where this work will lead me. At the moment it is for my own healing and preparation for doing Gods will. I trust that the way will be revealed in time.

Yes, I am sensing freedom from the past, i.e. thoughts from the past have lost their hold/power to paralyse me, keep me locked into the past. I do feel that this is about my healing at the moment, a preparation for something to come. I am not 'saving the world' and would say that I do not rescue my clients from their pain. I do make myself available to them and I do authentically rescue when required. Inauthentic rescuing, which I have done in the past is not only unhelpful to the client but myself as well as it would mean that I take on unnecessary responsibilities for the others well being. My soul journey is about 'serving ' others and I have learned how best to do this from mistakes. Of course I will make more, and this is how learning occurs sometimes. My current learning is that I need to take care of me so that I stay well and charged rather than sick and drained. This is about balance, and holding God and the angelic realm at the heart of everything I do, even more than I do already, much, much more, by allowing myself to be the channel for them to work through me whilst holding and seeing the Christ in the client. Last autumn I made a decision that I wanted to get closer to God and at that time was unsure about how to go about this. The course came at the right time and will help me to connect to my inner God centre, to listen to his will for me. The angels will guide and help me to do this. Now I know how to ask for guidance and instruction from the Angelic Realm. For example, during my quiet time last night I was told to read the book of Samuel in the New Testament. Samuel told ' the Lord that he was listening and the Lord began to give him messages. If you are really serious about wanting to return to the Lord, get rid of your foreign gods...determine to obey only the Lord, then he will save you. Talk with God and he will give you new attitude.' And I'm only up to chapter 12!! OK lord, I hear you. I am seeing what's behind the parables in a way that I have not seen before. Once I figure what my foreign gods are, I can let them go. That'll be tonight's question to the Angels!

I am certain that the next 6 months will be transforming for me and I have no doubt that I will be closer to God and his Angels a result. **Martin February '05**

A few words of feedback re sessions recently experienced from my point of view are certainly a deep feeling of peace when I was experiencing the treatment and a definite feeling of lightness especially after the hands and feet were massaged.

I received the 4 keywords in the session after we graduated ***RELEASE {NEGATIVITY} OPEN {THE HEART CENTRE}***
RECEIVE {DIVINE LIGHT AND CHRIST CONSCIOUSNESS} SERVE {THE CLIENTS AND TO BE A SERVANT FOR THE ANGELIC REALMS} all of which made sense at that time also a definite feeling of deep relaxation during and after the session and a feeling of liberation. Certainly I felt the monthly sharing between Sean's angels were essential in order to have continuity and support in the therapy practice, in order to exchange the healing and to practice the technique of giving the therapy to my fellow students.

Within the group definite sensations of different energies felt e.g. Cindy had seen a chalice overflowing, and a cross and also an angel I remember.

Angela had also experienced a deep feeling of healing and of empowerment, when receiving the treatment. Whilst I was observing Angela and Cindy practicing I was aware of a definite shift in the energy of the room in which we were in, and also I was aware of a physical sensation in my right temple which I recognized as a sign of the presence of angels because it was the sensation I was given during the course in August in the garden when you had set us the assignment connecting with the angels so I was aware of the energies of the garden and the angelic realm in nature. **Theresa *Dent TCCP February 2005.***

I had never heard of Therapeutic Touch or Channelling until a friend told me about Sean's work as a Healer and channeller using angelic love and light. The course has transformed my life to the point that I can breathe and let go and let my God/dess be. For years I was trapped by memories of sexual abuse and through the course I was empowered to look at my wounded child within and be set free! The last day of the course also helped me reclaim my inner being and permit myself to experience real joy and laughter again after 48 years of living in 'hell.' I was overwhelmed to meet my beautiful Archangel Metatron. At first I called him Ministroni but he knew what I meant! ***Aggie Scotland.***

Dear Sean, how good it was to see you and how blessed I was by your ministrations to me. I pray that your work will go from strength to strength and that many will find renewal and rebirth with your help and guidance.

I value your prayers and feel surrounded and upheld by prayer - what a wonderful power it is. I was reminded of the words of a hymn after your visit. " But His angels here are human, not the shimmering hallows above. And the drumbeats of His army are the heartbeats of our love." All my love ***Ada F. Preston, Lancs.***

Feedback from our from clients and our student therapists.
BEFORE

It was a busy Sunday afternoon, making Sunday dinner, ironing and doing general household chores. I was running on adrenalin and my stress levels were moderate, bearing in mind that I am a very nervy person as the norm.

DURING

I started off 'stiff' and jumpy as I find relaxation states difficult to achieve. In time I found I entered quite a deep relaxation. I felt unexplained changes in my heart rhythm...firstly a speeding up, then slowing. The anointing tickled at first and I wanted to giggle but found it very pleasant and relaxing. Even though the room was quite cool I noticed that Paula's hands were very warm. I assume that was energy.

IMMEDIATELY AFTERWARDS

I felt a bit 'woozy'. After a couple of hours I became unreasonably tired and couldn't keep my eyes open so had to go to bed very early and slept very deeply for about 13 hours.

FOLLOWING FEW DAYS

I suffer chest pains every day as a normal part of my stressful life, the chest pains completely disappeared and I generally felt more relaxed, laid back and able to cope with pressures.

Ann Maidment was given a therapy by Paula; this is her 'verdict'

Before coming up to see you I had a small doubt that I would be told my understanding is wrong but for the most part I was overjoyed and looking forward to what would take place like a child who can see the wonder of Christmas and your own birthday. For me the session was finding more understanding about myself and what I came to do. To be willing to be more excepting of myself and let the divine angelic work through me on a bigger scale let more of my essence through. During the healing I had the feeling that the confusion and negative energies were being lifted from my head down out of my feet. I was able once again to feel the unconditional love, calm, peace. I could see this energy, which was also in the house and garden at Chapel Gap in Storth. I felt connected to everything and a few days my joy was overflowing. It is now two weeks since I experienced my very first session of therapeutic channelling and I know over the past six months my body has been through a deep cleaning and healing process on all levels. I have now made decisions about my path for the next year, which is to do the work I have been asked to do. I now sense that I am being called to work with these sacred energies as a therapist of Therapeutic Channelling. I wish to say that there are no words that I could write to express this experience so truly no words are needed. You should experience therapeutic touch for yourselves. I am grateful each day that I have been able to see the truth and I know we are so blessed everyday. I have been asked to speak the truth and be myself.

Viv -Staffs.

To experience this therapy is to:

- Experience Divine Love.
- To connect with your God/Goddess.
- To feel the angelic energies.
- To be blessed and have there feet and hands anointed is something they will not experience in any other treatment.

The benefits:

- Being empowered to start healing themselves.
- To realise that they are a Child of God – and connect with that child.
- To release pain and anger.
- To relax.

Dear Sean, How good it was to see you and how blessed I was by your ministrations to me. I pray that your work will go from strength to strength and that many will find renewal and rebirth with your help and guidance. I value your prayers and feel surrounded and upheld by prayer - what a wonderful power it is. I was reminded of the words of a hymn after your visit. " But His angels here are human, not the shimmering hallows above. And the drumbeats of His army -Are the heartbeats of our love." ***All my love AF. Preston, Lancs.***

I have used the Therapeutic Channelled energies on 2 Reiki Masters. Both found the treatment to be very powerful –both could feel God and the angelic realms at work. There was a flash of 'white light' as the Divine came upon them. I have to say that it was beautiful to be a part of it. Both ladies had positive responses and are coming back for further treatments. *Bernie (TCCP). Mullingar. Co Westmeath. Ireland.*

Dear Sean, as promised a little ditty for our mutual appreciation society! No seriously I didn't know what to expect when I was on my way to you, all I knew is that I needed to come. I was welcomed so warmly and felt as though I had come home straight away. The food was heavenly the spiritual care and love shown to me divine. When you channelled the energies through me I felt blissful and peaceful but most of all really genuinely loved and blessed. A true gift thank you, you have touched my soul and I hope to return soon for a second helping of bliss. *Wendy X*

Dear Sean, Thank you (and Ellie and Winston) for welcoming me so lovingly into your home yesterday. The session was certainly beneficial for me. I have been blessed with some astonishing and deeply healing experiences over the past year at the same time as trying to embrace the damaged child inside myself. I feel like I am being `fast tracked` in my higher chakras, leaving the lower ones struggling to keep up! The painful lump in my solar plexus seems to have been there for aeons. I'm also having problems finding the right people to work with and assist me - I find a lot of the `spiritual men`* I've come across recently are so "up their own third eyes" they find my approach incomprehensible and, hence, myself unacceptable. Anyway Sean, you took me yesterday to the place yesterday where God lives ... and allowed me to receive the reassurance I was seeking. I knew when I first read about you in Kindred Spirit that you are a man of true Divine Heart - which is the place from which I naturally operate. You gave me beautiful confirmation and affirmation of my Self and I thank God for you and your blessed work. I'm sure that much will emerge from the session over the next few days/weeks. For now, I am focussing on becoming a `woman of prayer` as you advised me ... and a path I was enjoying until recently when one of the above-mentioned* belittled me for `worshiping something outside myself`!! Lord save us from `spiritual men`!!! heh heh heh :-) I will be in touch soon. Take Care of Your Self. Big Hug - ***Jude North Cumbria.***

Angelic Energies

To me they are of the most high vibrations.
They are soft, unconditionally loving and gentle.
They heal the essence of your mind, body and spirit.
They move with the GRACE of a butterfly
And hold the BEAUTY of a flower.
They are one with all you can see,
Which are also you and I.

The essence to be the energy that is you and I.
To feel and see them just be and look around you,
For what can you see.
Listen from within and you can hear them
Speak the truth of who you are.

If you ask they give so be open to receive.
Keep this connection and live in joy
And dance with them through life.
You can never be alone when you are a vibration
Of energy of the most high that is LOVE,
That is you and I from above, below,
And see who you can be.

This wonderful world is here for you and me.
Remember who you are,
You are one with all just like me.
So, in truth and integrity just be.

That's what the ANGELIC ENERGIES mean to me.

Vivienne Bell TCCP
4.4.04

Angels of God.

Angels of God are close beside YOU

Waiting in love
They are there to guide you.
When you ASK them to help you,
They will shower you with love
Because they already know you.
Seek first their path to true peace and joy
And know that they will sustain you
The Child of God you truly are.
Believe in your heart that when you summon them,
They will come to bless your life
Forever more.
Angels of God are here to stay,
So rest assured that they are with you now
All the way.

Dedicated to Ellen Ann (died 2002) an angel of God.
Sean Bradley.

Angels

Always
Near
Guiding
Everyone
Like
Stars.

IN CONCLUSION

This Therapy is compatible with almost all of world religions, and does not rely on Christianity. The Divine Energy and angels existed before the birth of Christ. (Christians believe in the Holy Trinity - comprised of The Father, the Son and the Holy Spirit). The Energy remains unchanged.

The Divine Energy and angels exist -unreliant of a belief in their existence.

In fact, more and more of the scientific community are coming back to the proposition that in the face of such a creation as the universe/ multiverse -- there MUST exist a Creator. On many fronts in the scientific fields, there are steps nearer to the proof of this. It is only a matter of TIME before proof is conclusive.

Who knows what exists between the molecules of a piece of wood-which was previously thought to be solid!!!

The Teachings of the Essenes provide a Divine Blueprint for a Therapy which speaks to the Human Condition and can **CHANGE LIVES** by teaching Man that by deviating from God's LAW, he is the cause of his own destruction, and that of his own Planet-(as described by our Scientific Experts).

Just by communing with the Angels and Nature Realm as God intended at the Creation, and by transmuting all negativity into Love, Man can HEAL himself, (as sons and daughters of the Creator) and his planet, and in doing so SOLVE WORLD PROBLEMS!

Sean Bradley has specially designed this course, to help to facilitate this, in reliance on the preceding information.

May the Angels of Light and Love dwell with anyone reading these words?
Jeanne Drinkel TCCP CTSBA

When you love should not say, 'God is in my heart,'
but rather, 'I am in the heart of God.'
Kahill Gibran

Section 6:

Sean Bradley Academy Courses

- Core Values of the Academy
- Letter from the Principal of the Academy
- Overview of our certificated residential and non-residential courses.
- The Introductory Angel Healing Course for learners.
- The Angel healing Day.
- The Beginner's Course for student therapists.
- The Advanced Practitioner's residential course at Chapel Gap.
- The residential Teaching and Practise course for qualified therapists.
- The Master's certificated course for teachers.

CORE VALUES OF THE TEACHING AND PRACTICE COURSE

The Sean Bradley Academy is a dynamic new entrant to the field of professional development in complementary therapies now incorporating Therapeutic Channelling of the Christ /Angelic healing energies. We strive for the highest possible standards in the training content and utilise leading edge delivery methods in a first class facility at our teaching centre in the South Lakes of Cumbria. Our overriding aims are:

- To ensure real and lasting learning is achieved and that student realise their full potential in their chosen fields of study.
- To provide a safe and supportive environment which allows learning to take place in a professional and calm atmosphere.
- To empower our students connect with their own divinity as a 'Child of Source,' through connecting with their inner core values and release and reconnect with who they truly are as Light Workers.

Our courses are usually recognised by the International Federation of Healers (UK) I.F.O.H. and draw heavily on both internal and external evidence based clinical practice. All materials are subject to stringent review processes, which include validation by our qualified Principal and founder, Sean Bradley.

All courses are backed up by high quality course materials, which are provided to students in hard copy. Multi-media techniques are increasingly used to enhance the learning experience in course delivery.

The Academy recognises that for many student /therapists, attending a training course can be stressful, so our premises are friendly and welcoming. Any concerns are listened to and dealt with quickly and empathetically.

Our trainers and teachers have all graduated from the Academy and their expertise is invaluable to our growth and future developments both locally and on the international stage. Our community of professional therapists and teachers is 'close knit' and focused on excellence. Continuous improvement and cross-fertilisation of ideas are important to us, as is consistency of information across courses. We draw upon a high calibre of qualified professional therapists from within the Academy itself. Our motto "Only the Best for the Best" speaks for itself and through 'word of mouth' our reputation is spreading as a leader in holistic/ healing therapies.

Letter from the Principal

Using the most powerful, yet gentle methods of Therapeutic Channelling and Sacred touch, I will open your hearts and souls to these sacred energies, that you may be empowered to self-heal all that is broken, wounded and in pain, preparing your path to Ascension. Everything given in Love & Light.

The Academy empowers **YOU** to experience **JOY,** sharing and reconnection with all that you truly are before sharing it with others /clients. We hope through our courses and products to empower you embrace the Christ Consciousness and prepare you for the eventful day – **21st December 2012 –5 D energy!**

Therapeutic Channelling, working in divine partnership with the Four Spheres of Angelic Beings is about being connected to and working from your 'Heart Centre,' working with the high vibrational healing energies of the Lord Christ and Mary Magdalene. Their combined essence of 'Love, Light and Compassion' will empower you to reclaim your divinity as a co-creator of the Divine.

I believe that each one of us is a 'Living Sanctuary, a Sacred Oasis' where sacred energies can touch our lives, empowering us to experience a spiritual and fruitful relationship with our God /dess and our higher-self.

Our Aims:

- To uncover the inner innocence and love of self through connecting with the Christ energies and also with the angelic realms of Light.
- To break down self-imposed barriers to regain inner freedom of self-love, through feeling and thinking through the 'Heart Centre.'
- To learn to channel the Christ (Xt.) and Angelic healing energies, through the art of touch to assist others in regaining their inner innocence of Pure Love-the core of their Being.

Overview of all our courses.

- Our certified courses are structured into modules aiming to re-connect the self with the innocence of inner Divinity and then learning to channel the Angelic & Christ Healing energies of pure Love to another, through the art of touch and sacred words from the heart. Our courses are aimed at those who are dedicated to finding their inner self of Love and are ready to undergo emotional change as they uncover their hidden potential of living through the Heart and the channelling of pure energies to assist others in self-healing.

I look forward to meeting you in the foreseeable future.

Yours in Angel Blessings, Love and Light.

Sean
(The Barefoot Angel Man).

Overview

Each one of us is called to be "***Inner Living Sanctuaries***" where Angels can touch our lives empowering us to experience a deep passionate, meaningful, fruitful and intense 'love affair' with our Creator God – with our 'Higher Self' and with our Angels.

To meet with our personal Angel usually we have to be broken! Brokenness leads us to wholeness and this in turn leads us to angelic awareness and blessedness.

In my faith journey I experienced a complete mental health breakdown in 1996, triggered by the adverse effects of Prozac. I lost everything! My home; my position as a senior nurse manager; my partner of 26 years my dignity; my freedom and my health.

My breakdown became my Breakthrough and it was during this period of what I call 'the dark night of the soul experience' that I became aware that my life was important and that our Angels had a specific plan for me – just like they have a plan for you!

We must be 'stripped bare' like the layers of an onion!

You too have a story to tell like me! Rather than dwell on the 'negative' I advise you to turn your life experiences around and open the eyes of your mind-body and spirit and see whom you really are! Your presence here is valued and you are precious not only to me but to the Creator and the Angels. Experience their unconditional selfless love for you today!

The Angels are messengers, used by the Creator, to touch us – to heal us – to restore us – to empower us to wholeness, inner peace and our ultimate happiness. It is not a sacrificial or superficial happiness! It is a deep abiding inner peace that transports us to a safe place where we can finally be ourselves and reclaim our unique gifting as co creators of the Divine. We arrive at our sacred oasis where we can respect and love ourselves and most importantly we can learn to forgive those who have robbed us unfairly; those who have raped our divinity, dignity and spirituality. Lastly, we are shown how to FORGIVE OURSELF in love.

If we cannot forgive ourselves, then how can we possibly forgive those who have hurt us – damaged us – raped us?

If I say to myself, “ I Forgive, but I cannot forget!” then we have not entered the spirit of Forgiveness and because of this I believe that I am truly not forgiven but trapped in my negative energy!

Forgiveness is also about letting go and letting God Be! Forgiveness is also forgetting who, what, why and the wherefores of the scenario surrounding unforgiveness and forgiveness! To be forgiven, we must understand the dynamics of forgiveness and BE!

Ground Rules for all Courses and Workshops:

- ❑ Be Respectful.
- ❑ Be Open.
- ❑ Be Honest.
- ❑ Be Selfless.
- ❑ Be Humble.
- ❑ Be Observant.
- ❑ Be Obedient to 'your inner voice.'
- ❑ Be Sincere.
- ❑ Respect Confidentiality.
- ❑ Respect another's Spirituality, Culture & Creed.
- ❑ At all times 'Be Yourself.'
- ❑ Be at Peace in your Sacred Oasis with your Angel.

Things YOU must do before a workshop begins:

❑ Turn up on time. If you arrive late expect to wait outside until the next interval / break.

❑ Switch off your mobile phone and leave it switched off when you are inside with the group.

❑ Respect SILENCE as it represents the presence of God and is considered to be the "Sister of God."

❑ Enjoy the experience.

❑ Nurture newfound friends and BE Yourself!

Everything given is given in Love

YOUR RESPONSIBILITIES AS A NEWLY QUALIFIED THERAPISTS

Your responsibilities as a qualified therapist, representing the Academy, carries with it great responsibilities that have been entrusted to you by the Divine. It is not by 'chance' that you came to us.

You were chosen by the Divine to speak their truth –empowering you to speak your truth to the world in love. Your mandate is to prepare others to embrace Christ Consciousness by connecting with all that they are as a *Child of God – a Co Creator of the Divine.*

As a Teacher working for and on behalf of the Academy, you are reminded of the word 'Commitment' and all that this entails for you both as a therapist and as a teacher of Therapeutic Channelling.

The words '*Physician heal thyself*' are words that you have already embraced during your training. Now we give you several more 'KEY WORDS' and they are, "*Practice what you Preach.*" Being a teacher is about being in service and drawing from the wealth of your life's experiences. The Academy is there to support you at every level of your new career, and empower you to grow as a child of the Light. Connecting and working from your 'Heart centre,' not your head will stand you well in the face of life's many challenges.

Remember, this and you won't go far wrong – your students are your teachers of your tomorrow and if you listen from a place of absolute integrity and love, there you will see the face of the Master.

I remain your in service to the Light

Sean

REFLECTION

(This was given to me in 1993 and it has stood me the test-during those difficult times when I thought all was LOST!)

Help Me to act justly –
to love tenderly
and to walk humbly before you
Lord.
Prophet Michah 6:8

"Preparing Yourself for 2012"

STUDENT'S
PRE-COURSE
INFORMATION BOOKLET

Residential 4 Day
Advanced Therapist's
T.C.C.P. Course

CHAPEL GAP
SOUTH LAKES
CUMBRIA
TEL: 01524-762292
www.sean-bradley.com

This is a **4-Day intensive** certificate Residential course designed for Practitioners who need to reconnect with their inner child and **RELEASE** all negative mind-sets before working with sacred energies with their clients. Each course is **'Channelled'** throughout and students are advised to come without any expectation **-just be and receive all that is given in love from the realms.**

The course is structured into 4 Modules aiming to reconnect the self with the innocence of inner Divinity and then learning to channel the Christ (Xt.) sacred healing energies with the Archangels & Angels energies of pure love to another, through the art of sacred touch and sacred words from the heart centre.

The course is aimed at those who are dedicated to finding their inner self of love and are ready to undergo emotional change as they uncover their hidden potential of living through the Heart Centre and the channelling of powerful energies to assist others in self-healing.

The course will empower you to connect with all that you truly are as a Child of Source working in partnership with the Christ /Angelic healing energies of the Four Spheres, underpinned by the teachings and philosophies of the Essenes.

St. Germain's message "there is no course to learn how to channel divine energy other than the cleanliness of one's own heart. So perhaps as such we should consider everything. Then balance and perfection will be in our reach."

This course has been designed to work with a much smaller group of 3-4 Therapists, providing a safe environment by creating the ideal setting to help each individual face their ghosts -Inner Child or other Core Issues and to move forward. This course is intensive with positive results for the student -the therapist -the group -the client.

The Day will start at:

8.30 - 9.15am	**Breakfast**
9.30am	Morning Seminar (1)
11am	Morning Break
11.15-12.45pm	Morning Seminar (2)
1 - 2pm	Vegetarian Lunch
2.00 - 3.00pm	Rest / Study Period
3.00 - 4.30pm	Afternoon Seminar (3)
4.30 - 5pm	Tea Break
5 - 7.00pm	Private Study Period
7.15 - 8.30pm	Vegetarian Dinner
8.45 - 10pm	Evening Seminar (4)
10pm - 10.15pm	Tea Break
10.20 – 11.25pm	**Group 'Quiet Period' with the anointing of feet in presence of Christ / angelic energies**
11.30pm	Retire in Silence

4-Day Residential TCCP Course

Please can you arrive, say before 6pm so that you can be introduced to the small group and join us for our evening meal at 7pm. The course begins at 8.30pm following dinner.

As we will be working in a shoe free room, please bring either warm thick woollen socks or slippers.

Re Diets: we will do all we can to accommodate your dietary needs. However, you need to tell us what you can and cannot eat so we can make your stay with us enjoyable and safe. Please bring with you any medication or supplements that you are currently taking. The responsibility now rests with you!

Re: Course materials: you only need to bring your Journal for personal notes. The course will involve private study and some homework that will involve listening to our in-house teaching series of CD recordings. So as to take part in the personal study and reflection part of the course, we recommend that you bring your personal CD compact disc player with headphones.

I look forward to welcoming you in the name of Divine love and I know that the Christ and the Archangel Princes have selected you to make this beautiful journey. Surprises and gifts now await you. All that we ask of you is that you are willing to come and explore the sacred healing energies through the eyes of selfless, unconditional healing love.

Yours in Angel Healing Love and Light.

"Prepare Yourself for 2012"

Sean Bradley Academy

4 Day Advanced Course for Practitioners
"Residential"

With
Sean Bradley Consultant, Healer, Author and Life Coach

Course: £
Includes all accommodation, meals and course materials.

Rediscover how the healing energies of the Lord Christ & the Four Spheres of Angelic beings can empower YOU to 'self heal' & re-learn how to love yourself.

BEHOLD – ENFOLD –HOLD – LISTEN
TO ALL THAT YOU ARE
AS A CO CREATOR OF THE DIVINE!

COURSE AIMS:

- To empower the therapists to face their Inner Child Core Issues and face their individual fears through the eyes of selfless love – thus empowering the therapist to 'self-heal –reclaim-and release their ghosts.'

- To uncover the inner innocence and love of self through connecting with the angelic realms of Light.

- To break down self-imposed barriers to regain the inner freedom of self-love, through feeling and thinking through the heart centre and not the 'head centre'.

- To rediscover how the healing energies of Christ can empower YOU to 'self-heal.'

- Experience the presence of Mary Magdalene and learn how to work with her sacred essence through touch.

- To learn to channel the Christ (Xt.) and Angelic healing energies, through the art of touch to assist others in regaining their inner innocence of Pure Love, the core of their being.

To embrace your inner child –and embrace all that you are as a child of God.
Your inner child is your teacher.

COURSE OVERVIEW:

The 4 day 'Advanced Course is geared for a small number of students (3-4) who are willing to undergo an intensive course as well as dealing with their inner child issues in a safe environment conducive to self healing in the presence of the healing energies of the Archangels Metatron, Michael, Gabriel, Uriel and Raphael.

The course consists of a 4-day intensive designed for Practitioners who are already working with sacred energies with clients. The final 4th day is a 'Retreat Day', which is taken on the last day of your 6-month probationary period followed by a presentation of your certificate of accreditation and acceptance into the Academy.

The course is structured into 4 Modules aiming to reconnect the self with the innocence of inner Divinity and then learning how to channel the sacred healing energies of Christ with the Four Sphere of Angelic beings using the Angel Bagua and Healing Trigram, using sacred symbols, touch, blessed oils and 'channelled words from one's Heart Centre 'Christ Consciousness.'

The course is aimed at those who are dedicated to finding their inner self of love and are ready to undergo emotional change as they uncover their hidden potential of living through the Heart Centre and the channelling of Christ's powerful energies to assist others in self-healing.

The course is unique! It challenges YOU to take back your control and personal power. During the 4-day course you are 'Affirmed' that as a co creator of the Divine, you are 'whole, perfect and complete.'

As a therapist, YOU are invited to embrace the teachings of the Essenes; their way of life and connect with your Heavenly Father and Earthly Mother by working in partnership with the Four Spheres of Angels.

FACILITATOR: SEAN BRADLEY

Sean is a Spiritual Life Coach, Healer, Teacher and author of several books and a series of personal recordings empowering many to embrace their God, personal Angel and child within. He is committed to supporting and empowering clients to experience inner peace, tranquillity and healing of Mind-Body-Spirit through one to one therapies or group work.

Born in Glasgow, Sean was brought up in Dublin. He felt that throughout his life he was being guided and that his life was mapped out. At the age of 16 he entered a monastic community and became a qualified nursing monk. Although he left the community when he was 24, he continued nursing for a further 30 years.

Sean now devotes his life to assisting clients to reclaim the dignity of their Spiritual Being by looking at the 'wounded child within' through the eyes of selfless love. Sean says, "I believe each one of us is touched by Angels, and we have within us, the gift of transferring their healing touch for the benefit of others." Known as the Barefoot Angel Man, Sean is perceived as the Therapist's therapist and healer. His natural abilities and sense of humour attract many to his inimitable style. Sean's humility and sense of spiritual direction and core values will touch your life. He practises what he preaches and lives a simple life of prayer, working from a place of absolute trust and integrity in service to the Christ /Angelic energies of the Four Spheres.

Come and see for yourself and experience a teacher with a different approach, connecting you with all that you tru are –a Child

COURSE CONTENT:

Module 1 (Day 1*): Connecting –Engaging –Working with the 4 Spheres of Angelic Beings through the Angel Bagua and Healing Trigram.* The Day is spent taking an in-depth view of the 'Divine Blueprint,' as another sacred tool that will empower us to work with angels – they with us and through us - how we engage with them and how we can connect with them / and they with us, as Channellers and facilitators of the Christ /Angelic healing energies preparing us in our Ascension and for **21.12.2012.**

Module 2 (Day 2): ***Theory & Practice of Therapeutic Channelling working with sacred healing energies through Touch*** using sacred oils to anoint the feet/hands and neck of clients. We focus on the 'Sacred Tools' that we need to empower us to heal self before channelling Divine love to others. We focus our attention on the 'gift of sacred touch' with practical demonstrations of the 'self-healing technique' used to unblock the '**Heart Chakra/Centre**,' before anointing each other's feet. During the 6 months probationary period of study, students are invited to meet up regularly to practice the therapy with each other.

Module 3 (Day 3): Spiritual Development Day reflects on your sacrality and divinity as a co creator of the Divine. The morning involves looking at one's inner child through the eyes of selfless love and connecting with the wounded child and releasing the blocks and taking back your 'Power & Control,' using powerful Affirmations to unblock negative mind-sets. In the afternoon, you are invited to work with the Tree Divas /Nature Spirits in the nearby woods,

Day: 4 (Final Day): (completed after a 6 month probationary period of training and supervision) is a special day spent in silent reflection and quiet prayer in the presence of the sacred healing energies of the Archangel Metatron; the Christ energies and the essence of Mary Magdalene. At the end of your 4th day, you are given your certificate and personal ID and accepted as a fully accredited and qualified TCCP Therapist of the Academy.

We recommend that you come to the course with no real expectations, other than to experience unconditional selfless love. Everything given is given from love –Divine Love –Channelled Teachings – empowering you to take back your 'control & personal power.' I believe that we who accept the Divine mandate to work with these sacred healing energies -

reinforces the theory that we were once members of the Essenes in a previous Incarnation.

Connecting with the Christ healing energies is taking playing an 'active part' in your Ascension

As a Channeller of the Christ /Angelic Healing Energies you become infused with the essence and sacrality of Christ Consciousness and that of Mary Magdalene -the one who anointed the feet of Jesus, empowering you to embrace the 'Oneness of God' in your daily life....

Course Criteria: That you have already completed our **Angel Healing Day Workshop,** and know about Archangels, Angels and their purpose particularly regarding healing energy. That you have either a relevant qualification/s in Health Care (Nursing), a recognised course in one of the Holistic/Alternative healing therapies; or a 'Hand's On' experience in caring for clients/others.

Completion of the Course:

That all new students to this course will agree to the following: Upon completion of the course modules, all candidates are invited to link up with each other and meet regularly. i.e. every 4 weeks.

At the end of your **6-month probationary period**, you will be issued with your Personal Identification Card and a certificate of achievement following your Residential 1 Day retreat at Chapel Gap.

Course Costs:

A deposit of **£000** is required upon booking course. 1st payment of **£000** is due 8 weeks before and final balance of **£000** due 4 weeks before course starts. This cost covers full board course fees and materials together with personal 1 to 1 tuition and supervision during the intensive course at Chapel Gap. The cost does not include travel. This remains your responsibility.

Bursaries: The Academy offers a 25%-75% Scholarships/ Bursaries to students who, because of their personal circumstances, are unable to meet the full costs of this course. All we ask is that you reciprocate an exchange of energy in a practical way! Please apply in writing explaining your circumstances. Your correspondence should be c/o Sean Bradley and marked "confidential". All bursaries are presented before the Angelic realms for their final decision. Payment by monthly instalments can be negotiated.

Your Commitment

When you sign our letter of Acceptance you are giving your consent To accept the strict conditions for undertaking the course.

Upon completion of the course, you will enter a 6-month probationary period of learning, supervision and support.

During your six-month probationary period of training, you will be invited to take part in our training events and gain additional hands on healing experience.

You may, from time to time, be invited by Sean to give a talk on your experiences of Angelic Energies at one of our Angel Healing Day Conferences.

Our Register of Safe Practitioners:

To remain on our register as a fully insured accredited **TCCP (Therapeutic Certified Channelling Practitioner)** you will have to undertake a firm commitment to keep yourself regularly updated as a therapist / Healer. It is recommended that you make a weekend /or 2 day retreat every 12 months as well as attending the 4 half-day study days in-house at Chapel Gap.

Insurance: If you are not already insured, we can facilitate insurance cover for you under our Block Policy with the International Federation of Healers UK.

AS A CHANNELLER /THERAPIST, YOU ARE THE BEATING HEART OF DIVINE LOVE IN A MODERN WORLD!

The Angel Healing Day:
(Non Residential)

Working with Your inner wounded Child.

The overall Aim of the 1-Day Angel Healing Workshop is to:

- EMPOWER you to identify with your Inner Wounded Child through the Heart Centre and not your Head Centre..
- Reconnect with your Inner Child through selfless love.
- Reclaim – Liberate and set free your Inner Child in the presence of unconditional divine love, the Christ healing energies.
- Experience the presence of Angelic Love.
- Embrace the healing energies of Archangel Metatron and the recently emerged Source Angel through meditations –silence – group work – sacred healing energies using sacred oils, incense, light and Therapeutic Channelling via Touch.

Overview of the Workshop:

You are invited by the Realm to spent this day in the presence of selfless, unconditional Angelic love working with the sacred healing energies of the Christ (Xt.), the Archangel Metatron and Source Angel.

You are encouraged to reach out and acknowledge the "Wounded Child Within."

We use the most powerful, yet gentle methods of Therapeutic Channelling and Sacred Touch that will open your hearts and souls to the Angels, that you may be empowered to self-heal, all that is broken, wounded and in pain.

This is a day for YOU. Everything given in Love & Light. A day of joy, sharing and reconnection with all that you truly are.

Angel Healing Day

PROGRAMME

10	Intros and Welcome
10.15	Ground Rules (Mobiles off / Respect for the energies and willingness to explore and receive Divine Healing combined with angelic healing energies. If you have to leave the group for whatever reason and you need help, please indicate by putting your hand up. Otherwise, I will know that you don't need assistance. The day is performed through love and a reverence for the Divine healing energies that are present.
Opening Prayer	
My Prayer.	
10.30	Morning Meditation " Meeting our Companion Angel".
11am- 11.15	Break 15 mins
11.30- 12.45	Morning Workshop See Questions
1-2pm	Lunch
2-2.45	Self-Healing Techniques.
2.45 –3pm	Quiet period to reflect.
3pm-	Candle ceremony
3.15-3.45	Closing Meditation. Angel Visualization of Px
4pm	Close /Finish.

What happens at a Sean Bradley Angel Healing Day?
An Angel Healing Day is a day where healing energy is released through celebration, joy, humour and laughter for those who are prepared to give of themselves.

Morning

After we introduce ourselves to each other I lead our **morning meditation** where we meet our personal angel and experience a spiritual uplift through peace and quiet. During our first workshop we reflect on the power of the spoken word and positive affirmations in a period of reflective silence. I try to empower each person to listen with their heart not their head. We try to re-programme the conscious mind, to educate the subconscious with positive affirmations, for example 'I am a child of the light', 'I am as good as I can ever be'. We then move on to look at 'what is an angel?' and share our responses in joy.

Afternoon

We move on to an exercise in self-healing. We look at simple techniques using the hands, listening to our hearts, focusing on quality and how to empower ourselves to self-heal and release negative thought patterns.

Our **candle ceremony** represents our gifts to the Universe. We exercise our free will, which is respected by the angels, and ask them for a message using the angel cards. We light our candles during a prayerful silence.

If you bring a piece of clear **crystal quartz** you can place this in front of the 'Channelled Paintings' of the angel of Source and the Archangel Metatron. These were painted by a dear friend Alison Knox especially for this workshop. The crystals absorbs the energy when we place them front of the painting.

We conclude the day with a **healing meditation** on the Angels Michael, Gabriel, Raphael Uriel and Metatron who will take us to the Source (the Creator). You will be invited to connect with your inner child and if wounded we are empowered to connect with?? And?? of that wounded child.

By the end of the day I hope you will leave with some important basic tools that are effective and which you can work with yourself each day.

Elaine Griffiths, Project and Co-Founder of The Monastery of St Francis & Gorton Trust & The Angels in Manchester, when talking about the early days of the Monastery said 'Along the way we have been joined by many like-minded souls who I'm sure have been sent to us by the Angels when the timing was right and their skills were needed the most. One of those special people was Sean Bradley who was introduced to me when he came to do an Angels Workshop in Gorton several years ago. Sean is a gifted and inspirational teacher who, through his gentle and humorous style creates a unique healing atmosphere for his audience. The Angels brought love, joy and laughter to Gorton that day and I felt privileged to be in their company.'

Positive Feedback

THANK YOU SO MUCH FOR TODAY. As a journalist, it's not very often I find myself stuck for words but somehow, I can't seem to find the Right words to express just how much I feel this has benefited me. Words don't seem to be enough somehow but it's been an amazing day And a truly wonderful experience. I can't remember the last time I felt this calm and chilled out but I can say that it feels really good. I feel an inner sense of peace within me, like I've got some clarity and direction.

I'd been feeling a bit lost and overwhelmed before but that really does seem to have lifted. THANK YOU. And it was a lovely group.

Having attended the workshop and experienced this amazing sense of inner peace within myself, I think I'll be able to promote future workshops in an informed way, as someone that has experienced the benefits first hand. Knowledge is confidence. I feel much more confident now in that I'd know what I'm talking about whereas I would have been a bit out of my depth before.

I am definitely going to set aside an hour everyday for my own quiet time (Spot permitting!!!!!). Today, at the workshop was The first time where I managed to switch off and remove myself from all the things that were going on around me in my life.

I feel that if I don't set aside some 'me time' on a regular basis, I'll forget how to achieve this calm so I'm definitely going to keep it up as it's done me the world of good.

Let me know if you have any events organised in Manchester so I can attend

Let me know well in advance if you have any events organised in Manchester
so I can help with promoting the event. It's important that I have the time
to plan any marketing and promotional activities properly.
Lots of love. Ramo in Manchester.

I have written much more about Angel Healing on my website: www.sean-bradley.com. I prefer to answer questions about angel healing and the workshops by e-mail but if you have read this far, you are obviously interested and I'd like to suggest you listen to your heart and come along to share with others who are interested and willing to share this experience.

COME AND SEE............................

FEEDBACK TO THE ANGEL HEALING DAY

My Dear Sean, Just wanted to let you know how I soooooooooooooo enjoyed the wonderful day meeting our beloved Angels and by learning and hearing your most special message, I now have the completion of my circle of knowledge for my future, your truth is my truth and our day was the missing link in my chain, I came home feeling so high and yet totally at Peace........... Thanks be to God !!!

I intend to have my very own Healing Sanctuary full time and it has to be in the States, I am using daily Affirmations to make this so, as I feel it is in my destiny to continue my work over there, however, somehow I have to come to your

Academy before the time is right for my next move.

I knew as soon as we met that you were to be the teacher who held the key to how I would continue on my Journey down my Path of Life. I just love the workshop C.D that I purchased, Heal Yourself with the Christ Energy. One of my Clients coming for Reiki Healing, who is very, very ill with breast cancer, came for a treatment and I did the meditation with her before starting the healing, my Guide had told me that it would be the perfect tool to assist her working with her very injured Inner Child, she had the most amazing Healing session after the Meditation and so I would love to do it again. If there is anything that I can do, please do let me know, in the meantime, can't wait to do more work with our Angels and I pray that you will always continue to be the very special Messenger that you are and I give thanks that I was Blessed with that wonderful day of learning and moving on with my Spiritual Journey.

For the time being I will close, wishing you and your partner much Joy and Happiness and loads of love and kisses to the four legged treasures, especially the little girl, she is such a cuddly little lass and reminds me of golden memories in my past.

God Bless, In Love, Light and Healing, My Love, ***Auriol. XXXKent UK***

The Introductory Angel Healing Course: <u>Working with the Angelic energies of the Four Spheres of Angels.</u>

The overall Aim of the Introductory Angel Healing Course is to:

- EMPOWER you to identify the names, titles, and positions of the Four Spheres of Angels.
- Be aware of what the Angel Bagua is and how you can use it.
- Explore the healing vibrational energies of the sacred colours of the Angel Bagua and Healing Trigram.
- Experience the presence of Angelic Love and Light.
- Embrace the healing energies of Archangel Metatron and the recently emerged Source Angel through meditations –silence – group work – sacred healing energies using sacred oils, incense and light.
- Identifying negative mindsets and knowing how to invoke and invite the angelic energies to empower you to release –reconnect and reclaim your dignity as a child of God.
- Rediscover how angelic energies can empower you to self heal through the use of positive Affirmations.
- Rediscover Therapeutic Channelling via Touch.

Overview of the Introductory Angel Healing Course:

You are invited by the Realm to spent 12 hours over 6 sessions in the presence of selfless, unconditional Angelic love working with the sacred healing energies of the Christ (Xt.), the Archangel Metatron and Source Angel.

You are encouraged to reach out and acknowledge the "Presence of Angelic Healing Energy in the Universe, the Landscape; the elements; the animal kingdom." The course will empower you to Invite –Invoke-Ask the Angelic realms to connect with you a Child of God.

We use a series of Sean's recordings from his "Angel Teaching Series" that will open your hearts and souls to the Angels, that you may be empowered to take the Beginner's Course that will eventually empower you to self-heal, all that is broken, wounded and in pain. The Academy will invite you to join us for the beginner's Course and become Channellers of Divine Love and Light (Christ Consciousness) working as a qualified Therapist TCCP.

This is a course for YOU.

Everything given in Love & Light. A course of joy, sharing and reconnection with all that you truly are.

Sean Bradley
The Barefoot Angel Man®

THE IMPLICATIONS OF THE COURSE

It is important that students take on board the **IMPLICATIONS** of what has been covered on the **INTRODUCTION TO WORKING WITH ANGELS COURSE.**

Of PRIMARY importance is the fact that as 'children of the creator'- you are a co- creator and as such you have the ability to ***heal yourself and other people***!

This ability to heal yourself however, - is totally dependent on your ability to ***forgive and forget***. If you are not able to do this, you cannot heal yourself -
as healing is blocked by the process of holding on to the hurt and pain that the person/situation has caused you.

That is why Jesus said 'forgive - not 7x 7, but 70 x 7 times.' It does not so much benefit the person receiving the forgiveness- (although, the positive effects can help them), so much as being of great benefit to the person doing the forgiving!

Another implication is concerned with the communions with Angels. Not only can you reap the benefits, which the Essenes reaped when you engage in this, i.e. - a longer, healthier life, but you can also ask for their assistance in more mundane tasks, such as helping you to find a parking space (if you have an important appointment), or helping you to achieve an important task or goal. Be assured that they are only too pleased to help you - if you ask!

Jesus himself said ' ***ask and it shall be given unto you'***. In fact, they are not allowed to help if you don't ask, as it could be seen as an intervention, and as such, possibly in contravention of your free will.

In addition to any health benefits which may be felt, the relaxation techniques and spiritual development which takes place over time, can help to promote an inner radiance which shines through, which cannot be achieved from the external application of any amount of creams and potions.

All the above takes is 'a leap of faith' to believe that all this is possible- and the world is your oyster - GOD WILLING!

“Beginner’s” Certificated Course

Therapeutic Channelling

Modules 1-6 Duration of Course 6 months’ probation.

With

Sean James Bradley

RGN, Therapist, Spiritual Life Coach,
Pastoral Counsellor, Author, Reiki Master, Trainer, Lecturer.

Member of the International Federation of Healers United Kingdom

The Beginner's Course

(non-residential)

THE COURSE MODULES:

Consists of 46 Hours learning over 6 full days. Probationary period – 6 months

MODULE 1:	Day 1.	***Come & Explore the Wonder of Angels.***
MODULE 2:	Day 2.	Introduction to Therapeutic Channelling with the Archangels Metatron, Source & the Angelic Realms of the Celestial Bagua & Healing Trigram.
MODULE 3:	Day 3 & 4	(2 Day Intensive Course) 14 Hours. **Therapeutic Channelling –theory and practice days**
MODULE 4:	Day 5	Personal Development Reclaim Your Dignity & Sacrality as a Co Creator of the Divine.
MODULE 5:	Day 6	Spiritual Development Day. (1 Day Workshop / Retreat) 6 Hours. • This is the final module of the Practitioners Course.
Module 6:		**Assignments and course work**

RETREAT PROGRAMME FOR CERTIFICATED COURSES

10.00AM	Welcome Address by Sean Overview of the day.
10.15:	The Teachings of the Essenes "Canticle of Mary" working with the Archangel Gabriel.
10.50am	Coffee Break
11.10	WORKSHOP: *The Essenic Canticle and its implications for you as a Light worker/Therapist.* Connecting with the Heart Centre.
11.50	Group Feedback to reflection
12.30	Lunch Break
1.45pm	Welcome Back
2.00pm	Workshop: TRUST ALL THAT YOU ARE:
2.40	Comfort break. (5 mins). Quiet Music
2.45pm	CANDLE CEREMONY.
3.00pm	ANNOINTING OF HANDS using Spikenard (Mary Magdalene) Concluding Meditation "Archangel Gabriel's invitation to you."
4pm	Sacred Dance 'Flaming Star.'
5.pm	Presentation of Certificates to Students.

Followed by Soiree & Celebration

Teaching

&

Practice
Certificated Course

In

Therapeutic Channelling

With

Sean James Bradley

RGN MASTER PRACTITIONER TCCP
Member of the International Federation of Healers United Kingdom

Sean Bradley Academy of Therapeutic Channelling for Practitioners

Student Application Form:

CONFIDENTIAL

YOUR SURNAME	
YOUR FIRST NAME/S	
HOME ADDRESS:	
E-MAIL ADDRESS:	
TEL NUMBERS:	
MOBILE TEL NO'S:	
NEXT OF KIN:	
CONTATC DETAILS:	
STATUS (married /single/ divorced)	
LIST ANY HOBBIES:	
DIETARY NEEDS:	
Other:	

INDICATE ANY RELEVANT EXPERIENCE YOU MIGHT HAVE HAD

____

____

____

____

____

____

WHAT DO YOU HOPE TO ACHIEVE FROM UNDERTAKING THIS COURSE?

____

____

____

____

____

____

____

IN THE SPACE BELOW, PLEASE ADD ANYTHING WHICH YOU HAVE NOT HAD THE OPPORTUNITY TO INCLUDE ELSEWHERE

ON THIS APPLICATION AND YOU FEEL MAY BE RELEVANT TO YOUR ATTENADANCE ON THE COURSE.

____

____

____

SHOULD THE COURSE ADMINISTRATOR BE AWARE OF ANY HEALTH DIFFICULTIES, WHICH THIS COURSE MAY CAUSE SOME PROBLEM? IF SO, PLEASE INDICATE.

____

____

____

DO YOU HAVE ANY PHYSICAL IMPAIRMENT, WHICH MAY REQUIRE SPECIAL NEEDS? IF SO, PLEASE INDICATE.

____

____

____

ALL APPLICATIONS WILL BE TREATED WITH RESPECT AND ANY INFORMATION YOU SUBMIT WILL REMAIN CONFIDENTIAL. YOUR ENQUIRY IS VALUABLE TO US.

____

____

____

____

We aim to reply to your application within 7 working days and we will inform you of the Academy's decision. If your application is successful, you will be sent a letter of acceptance for your signature. You are invited to sign and post this and return with your deposit.

Signature:______________________________**Date:**_________________
Yours sincerely

Sean Bradley RGN
President of the Academy

T.T.C.P. 6 MONTHS LEARNING CONTRACT

YOUR FULL NAME____________________________________

TCCP COURSE COMPLETED ON (DATE):_______________

To qualify for certification, the Academy now invites you to complete your **(IN-HOUSE) SIX MONTHS PROBATIONARY TRAINING** by making a firm undertaking to do the following:

- Provide the course Principal with an Evaluation of your Course.

- To keep in touch with the Academy on a regular basis and let us know how you are progressing, following the course.

- To meet up with your fellow students on a monthly basis to provide support and network with each other.

- To complete all 6 Assignments of Home Study, as stipulated in (Module 4) of the TCCP Reference Manual. The first Assignment is expected within the first 2-4 weeks of leaving Chapel Gap.

- From Months 2 –6 of completing the course, you are invited to complete the remaining 5 Assignments based on the "Angel Teaching Series of CD recordings 1 –5. Please write briefly from your Heart Centre. This is not an examination!

- To become a fully qualified TCCP Therapist, you must attend the 1-day retreat upon completion of your 6 months probation.

- As part of our commitment to your 'on-going' learning experience, the Academy will invite you to join us, from time to time, in assisting us at one of our courses /events.

Upon completion of the 6 months **(Probationary Period of Training),** the Academy will formally invite you as a fully accredited and qualified member /therapist. Upon completion of your 1-day retreat here at Chapel

Gap, you will be issued with your certificate and ID badge and given details of our in-house block insurance cover.

To remain an active Practitioner on our database, you are invited to undertake a 2-day retreat on the anniversary of your certification every 12 months. This can be done anywhere as long as you can show the Academy that you have fulfilled the criteria.

If you are in agreement to these Terms and Conditions, we invite you to sign this acceptance letter and a copy will be given to you as proof of your consent.

I AGREE TO ACCEPT THE TERMS AND CONDITIONS OF THE ACADEMY'S LEARNING CONTRACT.

Signed:______________________________ Date:__________________

Witnessed By: Sean J. Bradley RGN MIFOH
Principal

Signed:**______________________________** ***Date:*** **_________________**

Yours sincerely
Sean Bradley
Principal of the Academy

BOOKING INFORMATION

To secure your place on this course EITHER completes the on-line booking form on www.sean-bradley.com, OR Complete the form enclosed and send it to the address below together with the deposit.

Sean Bradley Academy
Chapel Gap, Storth Road, Storth, Milnthorpe, Cumbria.
LA7 7JL. United Kingdom.
Tel: 01524-762292
To find out more about Sean please visit the website:
www.sean-bradley.com

On receiving your application we will send you confirmation of your booking and details of the venue and arrangements for the course..

On completion of this intensive course, you will be presented with course manual, set of teaching tapes. Your certificate will be given on your final day at the end of your 6-month probationary period of training.

We reserve the right to amend the arrangements where it is found to be unavoidable or to make other minor changes that may be necessary due to unforeseen circumstances.

The information about yourself that you give us is confidential and will be treated in accordance with the Data Protection Act 1988. Information will be processed primarily for keeping you informed of our courses and workshops. If you do not wish to receive information about future events, please contact us.

PAYMENT BOOKING TERMS AND CONDITIONS

1.DEFINITIONS

(a)"the company" shall mean Sean James Bradley trading as Sean Bradley Academy whose registered office is situate at: Chapel Gap, Storth, Milnthorpe, Cumbria LA7 7JL and his employees, agents and assigns;
(b) "the customer" shall mean the person, firm, company or other organisation with whom the Contract is made;
(c) "the Contract" shall mean the agreement between the Company and the Customer for the booking of the Training on the date and at the Venue as described overleaf;
(d) "the Training" shall mean the training or course booked by the customer as described overleaf;
(e) "Venue" shall mean the venue or location where the training is due to take place or such other venue as the Company and the Customer may agree in writing.

2. GENERAL

(a) These conditions shall apply to the Contract to the exclusion of any other terms and conditions or referred to in any order, letter, contract or other communication sent by the Customer to the Company and the express provisions of these conditions
(b) Headings are for reference only and words in the singular shall include the plural and vice versa and references to any gender shall include the others.
© Any concession made or latitude allowed by the Company to the Customer shall not affect the strict rights of the Company under the Contract.

3. PAYMENT TERMS

(a) The Customer agrees to make payment according to the price agreed, method and time of payment as stated overleaf.
(b) The Time of payment shall be the essence of the Contract.
(c) Deposits shall only be refundable at the discretion of the Company.
(d) All payments shall be made in Pounds Sterling unless otherwise agreed in writing with the Company.

4. BOOKING TERMS

(a) Bookings may be made provisionally but will only be held for a period of 21 days after which time they shall be deemed to be automatically withdrawn if the Company has not received a completed, signed and dated Booking Form from the Customer together with any deposits payable to the Company also reserves the right to cancel the Customers place(s) on any

Courses booked if the deposit payable is not received on or before the date agreed in the Contract.

(b) Bookings shall be confirmed by the Company following receipt of a completed Booking Form which is signed and

dated together with/following receipt of the deposit on or before the date agreed in the Contract.

shall apply unless expressly varied in writing and signed by Sean James Bradley of the Company (d) The Company shall use its best endeavours to provide the Training requested by the Customer but reserves the right to either cancel or rearrange the Training if necessary due to illness, accident or other circumstances beyond its control.

5. CANCELLATION PROVISIONS

(a) Once the Company has received a completed signed and dated Booking Form from the Customer, the Contract cannot be cancelled by the Customer unless the parties agree in writing and upon payment by the Customer of such amount as is necessary to indemnify the Company from all losses resulting from the said cancellation.

6. CUSTOMER SPECIFICATION

(a) The Company shall not be liable for any matter (including but not limited to the nature of the Training), which is due to or caused by any inaccuracies in any specifications or request supplied to the Company by the Customer or any failure by the Customer to make such request or specification.

7. FORCE MAJEURE

(a) The Company may delay or cancel the Contract and any course booked if and to the extent that the Company is unable to provide the Course as agreed due to illness, accident, delay or strike in the public transport, breakdown or other circumstance beyond his control.

8. JURISDICTION

(a) This Contract shall be governed by the laws of England and Wales whose courts shall be the only courts of competent jurisdiction.

“Only the Best for the Best” speaks for itself and through ‘word of mouth’ our reputation is spreading as a leader n holistic/ healing therapies.

Course Testimonies

I send my love. I know what is written is blessed and you can use it for the highest good. I am honoured that it was given to me. My three days on the course were "Wicked, Awesome, Cool" in the most delightful way.

I was shown "*Synchronicity, Humility, Joy and Selflessness*" by my brothers and sisters on the course.

Here are some of the words I was given to write and say during my stay on the 3 day advanced residential course:

- Healing releases love.
- Guidance creates release.
- Readiness for peace and wonder.
- Give glory and praise to the light.
- Enlightenment empowers our empowerment.
- Living shows you free uncontainable peace, with wholeness for fulfilment.
- This is the icing on the cake, the glue that holds it all together.
- I know I relish to just be.
- Together magic and excitement is born.
- I accept that my heart holds my joy, love, abundance that is my being.
- Our lessons of self give us experience with divine purpose of all that is; love to accept who we have always been –the grace of being present, which is.
- Acceptance of endless beauty leaves you speechless.

The energies are soft, caring and gentle –the most powerful and have no agenda or attachment just unconditional selfless love, balance, joy and peace. Which brings healing to you innermost a gift for you and you alone. You know it is a safe place to let go and just be.

OUR QUIET TIMES

Day One:

I could feel and see the energy and I was loved and at peace in a place where I was totally free and I danced the most infinite beautiful exquisite dance we will ever see. I was one with all. I was empowered with total freedom. I floated effortlessly. I could feel energy moving through my body being filled with love and light like lying on soft cushions on a warm bed.

Day Two:

I danced pirouettes with energy like a graceful ballerina on pure white ice. Then the energy flowed down my body like a cascading waterfall, which then turned into a spiral of pure white light, which moved in to a wave around me. I felt like an innocent child being rocked, encircled with love.

Day Three:

I feel like pure white light cascading down from heaven like a ribbon as entwined with my being. I am that effortless floating butterfly who is free that as vivid, bright colours that reflects and shines divine energy, which holds and stains my being. I dance in this exquisite light with balance and fulfilment not longing. My gifts fall from my wings to all living things around me. I sit on a beautiful flower that holds pure endless love, wherever I am I breathe in pure joy in return for being me, exquisite I am perfection this is.

TO EXPERIENCE THIS THERAPY IS TO BE ON EARTH AS IT IS IN HEAVEN WITH FREEDOM TO BE.

I would just like to say how I see myself as others and I send to you all the things I was given with love to those who were present and took this journey with me now –and before –and to who may ever read these words in the future. Sean, dear one, the energies will bless you more each day!
Love, Light and twinkles. **Viv (Derby –UK)**

It was for me the first step towards the rest of my life. ***B.M. / Ireland.***

I can now begin to see the meaning and purpose of Angels in my life as a therapist and healer. ***John/ England.*** Therapeutic Touch is for me a coming together with trust between two people / to know you feel loved and safe. **Bernie, Mullingar.**

Channelling is a wonderful gift given by God. The channeller is a sacred tool for the Divine love of God/dess -the sacred energies work through from the Divine to the channeller to the client- each client may feel a different feeling. **Sian Wales**

During the hands on approach my feelings are: I feel the love of the Divine God/dess in my heart -its as if my heart and soul are one bursting with love so strong all you want to do is share it with clients so they too can find great love and happiness. **Kath UK**

The benefits are that the clients can relax. They experience deep peace within themselves, which helps them restore their lives. They can learn to trust and thereby love themselves again and with this comes the love of their God/dess, which helps us to love all people again. **Robie UK**

As an accredited and certified Therapeutic Channeller I belong to God -my mind-my body- my spirit and most of all my soul. By the divine light of God I lead my life. I ask to see as He/She sees to feel as He /She would feel to touch as He / She would touch to be empowered with a deep passionate love to love God's people as he / She would like them to be loved. **Bridget Eire**

To protect the gifts of the sacred energies that are inherent in Therapeutic Channelling I have discovered how to 'ground myself,' night and day! The course has empowered me to be silent and listen to the sacred voices and be still. I pray for spiritual guidance in my sacred place and often through the day. My physical spiritual, mental balance I work on by praying and asking the Angels of the Healing Bagua and Trigram to help me while I grow and sow God's seeds. **Monica. Ireland**

Having completed the 5-module course I have been Reawakened- Re-affirmed – Empowered*!* **JC Manchester.**

The course has given me the strength to take the penultimate step of faith and look at my life as the Rescuer and face the wounded child within through the eyes of selfless love and be healed myself. **SBM. Dublin.**

Through knowing Sean I found my First Love! Not my boyfriend but my beloved Creator God/dess who formed me in my Mother's womb and now I am FREE. **HJV. Northumberland UK.**

I have been moved to the point of tears for the years spent in selfish activity and denial of my true feelings and needs as a Healer and Therapist. Now, I can see for the very first time and can really love and enjoy working with these sacred energies in the knowledge that I AM LOVED unconditionally*!* **Sally M Blackpool. UK.**

As a Channeller working in Partnership with Metatron, Source and the entire angelic realms I know that I am loved -chosen and called by name to touch others in the name of selfless love divine. Thank you. **Maria Cumbria.UK.**

The course has been a tonic! It's challenged me to look at myself and face the hurts and brokenness that have prevented me living life to the full as a human being and as a therapist! **Joe London. UK.**

I had never heart of Therapeutic Touch or Channelling until a friend told me about Sean's work as a Healer and channeller using angelic love and light. The course has transformed my life to the point that I can breathe and let go and let my Goddess be. For years I was trapped by memories of sexual abuse and through the course I was empowered to look at my wounded child within and be set free! The last day of the course also helped me reclaim my inner being and permit myself to experience real joy and laughter again after 48 years of living in 'hell.' I was overwhelmed to meet my beautiful Archangel Metatron. At first I called him Ministroni but he knew what I meant! **Aggie Scotland.**

Attending the course was unlike any other course I had been too! The energies were perfect and the group were ordinary people, some with their heads trapped yet searching for a meaning and a purpose to their personal lives and looking for a new way of connecting with their clients. Sean taught us to combine humour with laughter as well as nurture a sense of the divine energies and sacred influences in our work as potential channellers. I learned practical skills that I could develop and put into daily practice as a therapist with my clients and students. I recommend the course for beginners but be warned that blocks have to be removed particularly in Module 4. The group supports you to do this and the sense of belonging is wonderful. **Trisica Notts.**

I enjoyed the advanced 3-day course for practitioners as it empowered me to develop an ancient skill that has been in circulation for centuries. **Josephine Tulle. N.I.**

Working long hours as a therapist prevented me getting into a support group. Having completed the course in Ireland in August 2003, I am delighted to be a part of a loving family of fellow therapists. When I hit rock bottom they are there to help me cope. We meet up fortnightly and share the joys as well as the sorrows! Thanks everyone! **Angie BK Co Wicklow.**

Up until very recently, I was always giving to the point of denying myself! The course in Therapeutic channelling has empowered me to be more selfish and in a strange sort of way, I have been made aware that I too have specific needs as a human being. As a therapist caring for others I have been warmly accepted as a valued member of the Team of therapeutic channellers and when we meet up we truly enjoy being a part of a living group who know how to care for each other. **Jo S. Midlands. UK**

As a qualified nurse of many years, I have given to the point of exhaustion and despair! My taking this rather different course was indeed unique and challenging in many ways that I expected. My head was firmly wedged! Sean did know how to challenge me and I will never forget a favourite saying of his "the planet your anus and the planet tonsils." He was trying to tell me that so many therapists and specialists have their heads wedged between these two planets! How right he was! A wonderful course and I cannot find the words that best describe how it touched my Mind, Body and Spirit. **Jo Anne. Yorkshire**

It is refreshing to be a part of something vibrant and healing as Therapeutic Pathways Consultancy. The 6-day course touched a lot of painful memories that needed healing before I could move forward as a therapeutic channeller. "Physician heal thyself," will forever remain with me from my time on the course. How true it was then and more importantly now! We cannot touch another's life until we have been healed-restored and resurrected ourselves. **Jenny T. Cambridge UK.**

As a registered healer and Reiki Master for several years, I came to the course trapped and unsure whether I wanted to be involved in the healing ministry. Over the period of several months I completed the 5 modules and what an experience! Instead of feeling isolated and threatened by my many fears and insecurities, I was assured and empowered to 'let go' and be myself! Now, my life has completely turned around and for the very first time in my life, I can begin to see a meaning and a specific purpose for my being here...I never knew much about sacred energies or 'selfless love' until I had my feet anointed with sacred oils. Suddenly I experienced the Christ Energies in the presence of the Archangels. Not having a clear knowledge of Christianity - I am overwhelmed with the presence of the healing energies of Christ the Holy One! Thank you so much Sean for sharing your life and talents with one who will never forget the time spent with you and the group at Chapel Gap in beautiful Storth. I am so pleased that you continue to work with smaller groups as opposed to large groups. **Caroline B x Offaly, Ireland**

Straight away Sean made all of us feel at ease in explaining what the course entailed over the 3 modules split into 4 days over a course of months. To be a good teacher one has to be sympathetic, be able to empathise and able to converse with anyone on any level. Sean did all of this and more. His way of putting things across was so simple but powerful. His voice was soothing and relaxing. God always says that we should shine our light so that others may see. Sean's light shines brightly but with the pure light of unconditional love, honesty, healing and compassion. The course was an opening of a brand new beginning in my spiritual pathway. Many questions that had been left unanswered all these years have finally been answered. My togetherness with God, mankind and mother earth has become stronger and my faith restored. I always knew that on this mother earth we all have a purpose. Through this course it has made it more clearly in what mine is. The course showed me the difference between something idealistic and what really is realistic. I finally found again the child within me. To become as one with God and mankind one has to become a child again. For in becoming the child you find the purpose, the reason why we are here on this mother earth. You find your true inner self, the light no longer is a flicker it becomes a radiant flame that shines brightly. Not only touching one's life but others in the process. On each module I thought you could go no further in finding one's self. How wrong I was. I found memories hidden away, the hurt, anguish, confusion, pain and sorrow. Through the course it not only healed us on the outside but also on the inside, but more so, our spirit. My faith became stronger and my purpose in life became even clearer. I have always believed we are here to help each other with unconditional love and no strings attached. It's in the doing that counts and not what one can make from it. The course was so uplifting, so encouraging and so knowledgeable. ***In the spiritual pathway you walk, many people come into your life. Some touch your heart, some your soul -Sean did everything in love.*** **Maria London**

My personal comments about the course are, at the outset, it appeared daunting, but, as it unfolded and I began to see results, and feel very profound changes within, it was worth it. The course was skilfully planned so that I did the work myself rather than being 'spoon fed' information; this made the whole experience deeply personal and highly effective. Exhausting, but in a good way. The structure and course content were varied and each element was challenging. The variety was perfect and beautifully balanced between work (CD's) /Angelic connections (questions) and group work – I found the group work highly valuable as it was at those times that I had my biggest realizations. Mealtimes were wonderful bonding moments. The challenge was not a threatening challenge, more of a personal challenge, more of a personal challenge to open myself to myself and to the Divine, and also to see if I had the courage to deal with my 'shite', to look it in the eye and face it. I found Sean loving, gentle, warm, humorous, welcoming, approachable, a gifted and talented teacher /facilitator / mentor with a clear vision. Firm, in the gentlest way. My personal recommendations about the course that would benefit others would recommend that those embarking on this powerful course has to be 'in the right personal place' to reap maximum rewards from the course –but I trust the Realms to call the right people. Have I achieved anything from the course? A whole new lifestyle. Appreciation, clarity, enlightenment, awareness, purpose, an open loving heart; love; new people in my life to love; realization and a stronger connection to the Divine (and a thicker waistline!!) I would most definitely recommend this course to others. I agree it was totally right to keep away from the reference manual until home time –us 'head people 'can't be trusted' with the things to read and think about on our own!! Would I change anything, add anything or take anything away? No! I would recommend that those who take this course, take a couple days off after the course to rest and assimilate. **Paula. Manchester. February 2005**

The Introductory course is based on the preceding information. It is practical, in that the information will give the student some background knowledge about Therapeutic Channeling in general, as well as the benefits of, and how to go about working with the Angelic Realm.

A course that will 'stretch your mind' and re-awaken your 'Heart Centre'. **Gwynedd. London.**

The course was very profound in the way Sean channels these sacred energies to awaken the core of the inner self –that essence of pure love. Breaking down barriers of thought patterns and inner 'wounds' to heal the self and then learning to channel these energies to another through the art of touch using sacred oils. **Carol. Cumbria.**

"They put fresh heart into the disciples, encouraging them to persevere in the faith." Acts 14:22. Those words spring to mind as I reflect on the weekend that I spent in Chapel Gap doing Module 3 of the Therapeutic Channelling course. I feel refreshed, revived, empowered –more alive and full of joy that at long last I have found somebody. That just doesn't know what they are talking about but they believe it and live it too. Thank you Sean. **Anthony. Sligo, Ireland.**

Dear Sean, I was thrilled to see and meet up with you. You are truly an Earth Angel of service. God bless you. I though what I could do for you is take an excerpt from my new book on angels about you and list your website and mention the Angel Bagua and healing Trigram that you shared with me here in America. I would love to be a messenger for the angels about your beautiful service. Love **Rev Jayne Feldman USA.**

Thank you so much for your encouragement and support. The photo of Archangel Metatron is beautiful. Your prayers and practical support have really helped me cope. I have sensed the presence of our angels and know that I am being protected. Its good to know that there are people like you who are there

24-7. I cannot thank the angels enough for what you have done for me during this time. **Dorrett. High Peak District.**

Dear Sean, thank you so much for yesterday at the Angel Healing Day in St Helens. I awoke at quarter to one this morning, feeling very peaceful and knowing that you had been praying for me. The following statements came to me: 'no matter what happens now, I'm safe and strong'. 'The pain is about feeling safe to be alone'. 'I have been touched at Source'. (Thank you Metatron and Source). Thank you so much Sean. With love **Carol. Warrington.UK.**

Dearest Sean It was so nice to meet Angela again after so long. We met in Edgeworthstown, Longford yesterday and I had a Therapeutic Touch healing....absolutely amazing. Caroline did it for me and I must say....it did me the world of good. Absolutely amazing. So relaxing and grounding...which was what I needed. Well done for being the innovator of this wonderful therapy. **Grainne. Dublin Ireland.**

Thanks so much for making us so comfortable this weekend. Our stay with you was tranquil and peaceful. The sacred healing energies were truly present at Chapel Gap. Know words can best describe the overall impression of our experiences at Chapel Gap. Thank you for everything. We returned home feeling the benefit for our short break at Chapel Gap. **Jen. Hebden Bridge UK.**

The Angel healing day was profound. The pure honesty of the participants including yourself, Sean. It was a huge part of my spiritual journey, which certainly opened up doors for me with regards to the Angelic Realms and the healing process. Also, it was a safe space, where even participants could sing! Also Sean's gentleness and compassionate nature touched me deeply. I also felt a huge connection with Sean and admired his professionalism with answering our questions and presenting the information through a series of visual displays. I felt a great sense of relief that I was able to open up with like-minded people, who did not judge me. There was a wonderful sense of peace in the room and it stayed with me for some time. Sean is a truly wonderful charismatic individual who through working with the angelic realms shows himself to be a perfect example of what Earth Angels are about! His presentation skills along with his total professionalism about what he does, is second to none. However, it is his gentle, soothing, caring voice and compassionate nature, which shines though on the day. I would have no hesitation in recommending anybody to attend one of Sean's workshops. **Grace. Ireland**

Just like to say many thanks for your angel healing day workshop held in Carlisle on the 23rd of Nov. It was wonderful and my friends who came with me thought so too.. Yours sincerely. *Kathy Cumbria.*

Having attended at least half a dozen different workshops and courses which Sean runs, I am no nearer now to describing the mechanics of exactly what Sean does, than I was after the first one! I just know that along with marriage and childbirth, they have been the most amazing experiences of my life! In a world in which a smile no longer has much 'street cred', these courses invoke the higher aspects of life and can permanently enrich it immeasurably. Seek and you too shall find! **Jeanne Drinkel (St Helens Merseyside UK).**

Personal Reflections about Today.

People are often unreasonable, illogic and self-centred.
Forgive them anyway!

If you are kind, people may accuse you of being selfish, and having ulterior motives.
Be kind anyway!

If you are successful, you will win some false friends, and some true enemies.
Succeed anyway!

If you are honest and frank, people may cheat on you.
Be honest anyway!

What you spend a lifetime building, someone could destroy over night.
Build anyway!

The good you do today, people will often forget tomorrow.
Do good anyway!

Give the world the best you have, and it may never be enough.

Give the world the best you've got anyway!

You see in the final analysis, its between you and God.

It was never between you and them anyway!

Taste and see that the Lord Christ is good for your being.

What Angels have to show us as Healers & Therapists?

The angels of the Christmas and Easter stories are not absurd, for the Spirit that fills holy Seasons like Christmas and Easter helps us realize that life and living are not as simple as we sometimes think.

We realize that we are surrounded by mysteries and marvels so great that they can make even us change our lives.

We may recognise that we need to Love one another as the Holy One loves us; this can force us to a new way of life.

When we remember and relive the events of Bethlehem, Gethsemane, the Holy Sepulchre, the powers of Heaven come close to us. The veil that separates us from the world of the Spirit is drawn back.

Whenever God breaks through, we are surrounded by angelic powers.

There are numerous well-documented testimonies of actual events recorded in the scared books of the world's religions when angels touched the lives of ordinary people.

For the religious leaders & their doubting believers who deny the very existence of angels I would refer them to reflect on the important fact that angels did appear 384 times in the Christian Bible.

We don't have to be a Christian to believe in angels. Angels can touch our lives regardless of one's religious persuasion or belief. In my experience working with a diverse group of students, that I am amazed to see students who not practice a religious belief and who are completely open to these sacred energies experience the presence of angels!

For the writer's of the New Testament, the difficulty and challenge before them was to find a way to express the uniqueness of this man Jesus, to find words to convey the depths that they say in his death and resurrection.

In His selfless death, they knew that in Him the love of God had come among human beings in a remarkable way. They knew that God the Creator Being in Christ was reconciling the world to himself.

The stories of the angels in the life of Jesus do this: they have power which no lecture or broadcast could ever have.

When we read the story of His birth of a virgin mother, it speaks to us of the utter kindness and generosity of God, and of His creative power, which can draw new life out of empty wombs and barren tombs.

When we read the story of the turmoil this child brought into people's lives- Mary, Joseph, the Magi, Herod, the whole of Jerusalem and all the babes of Bethlehem – we are forced to ask ourselves whether the Risen Christ challenges and moves my life in the same way.

When we read the story of the shepherds and their vision of angelic choirs, we discover anew that in Christ, the prophet / Holy Man, the heavens open and our God /dess breaks into my life.

When we read the story of the message from heaven, of the glory in the highest and peace on Earth, we hear an echo of the Risen Christ who said just that to his disciples: "Shalom, my peace I give to you."

The Creator God /dess who made each one of us in love continues to say that to millions of His followers since. It's through these stories that a loving Creator God /dess continues to come to each one of us today and invites us to become a part of the story of His Life.

Our Christmas hymns describe a world more fully real than the materialistic world in which so many of us have been brainwashed. The drama of Christmas may well be giving us one of our deepest glimpses into the 'Heart of our God /dess.'

The Incarnation is a challenge to our way of life. It is in the cry of the poor the Christ still calls us; in the call of the other that He comes to us.

David Adam

What do Angels teach us today?

If the angels teach us anything, they show us what it means to put on the mind of our Creator God /dess when using the Christ (Xt.) energies.

What a great privilege is theirs, to stand constantly in God's presence, to feast their full eyes on Jesus and all the Holy men and women of ancient times to the present day.

The angels witness the inner beauty and wholeness of God. They feast their eyes on the face of Christ, to know his face and even more, His mind. They look upon all of the Ascended Masters – upon the world, and on each one of us, with the mind of Christ and of the Creator God /dess.

To truly love someone is not only to adore their face and their external reality and beauty, but also to enter their mind and heart.

To have the mind of Christ the healer is not a boast but a prayer, and the prayer is that we, more and more, learn to think God's thoughts and to see the world around us through the eyes and mind of God.

As Christians, we have not only the spirit, the love and the strength of Christ. We also have been given his mind. For those of you who are not Christian but who believe in a spiritual Being or God, you too take on the mind and heart of that living deity.

To truly love and care deeply for someone is not only to adore their face and their external reality, but also to enter their min d and heart. Like the butterfly that is drawn to the "beautiful," so are we drawn to their inner beauty?

To have the mind of God is not a boast but a prayer, and the prayer is that we, more and more, learn to think God's thoughts and to see the world around us through the eyes of God. We have not only the spirit, the love and the strength of God. We also have been given his mind and consciousness.

Our minds as well as our emotions are to be trained to see and judge the events of our day. That is why we are invited by the Scriptures and Holy Books to discern the signs of the times. We must prevent negative forces and influences from sapping our positive energy thus leaving us spiritual cripples with a hopeless dream.

There are many soothsayers who profess to know the answer to everything and who in fact know nothing pertaining to the truths of God. There are many false prophets who take your money and leave you bewitched, confused and deeply unhappy in your search for meaning and purpose to life's hurts and greater mysteries.

Be still and listen to that inner small voice deep within your Being. Get back there and stay there!

If your inner voice is restless and causing disquiet within your spiritual Being – then know that the voices you hear are not of God or from your personal angel but from forces working in opposition to spirit. Discernment of such destructive voices working in opposition to Spirit comes through enlightenment and through daily conversations with your God /dess and with the angelic realms.

These voices are from a place we call the 'dark side,' or that place where only conflict and chaos thrives leading to your ultimate destruction.

The spiritual forces that come from the dark side or opposing factions against God will try to deceive you by inviting you to follow them and disregard your higher self.

The easy way out is often the road to your destruction and downfall. The world we now live in demands instant remedies, solutions and answers.

It is not modern or fashionable to opt out of mainstream society and live by a unique code of standards that promote inner peace and solace connecting you with your Divine God. It is fashionable to wear the current fashion trends and go with the flow! It is not fashionable to be the odd man out as peer pressure dictates.

Silence is the true sister of the Divine. It is God who embraces you in Love in your silence today and everyday of your entire existence.

Your wishes to engage with God and the angelic realms are respected. You can choose to listen or not to listen. Your freewill is acknowledged and respected.

When we reflect on God's beauty as evident in the landscapes, art music, poetry and architecture we take on a different vision of our spiritual legacy handed down to us from our ancestors.

How often do we hear, "I don't want to look at the world through any lens at all, especially angelic ones: I want to look at all the facts and let them speak for themselves." This is the great heresy of our times: the myth of objectivity - the belief that the factors of life around us need no interpretation.

Anyone who brings some prior conviction into play is accused of ignoring or distorting the facts. There is no such thing as purely objective judgement. We all bring some lens through which to see the facts.

The angels have much to teach us. They offer us ways of looking at God – Christ – the Prophets – Holy Men and Women who have inspired our faith journey as Light Workers and at the world.

The angels teach us about simplicity, about delighting in God's presence. Responding to the question, "who was the greatest, Jesus, called a child," whom he put among them, and said, "Truly, I tell you, unless you change and become like little children, you will never enter the Kingdom of Heaven. Whoever becomes humble like this child is the greatest in the Kingdom of Heaven. Whoever welcomes one such child in my name welcomes me. Take care that you do not despise one of these little ones; for, I tell you, in Heaven their angels continually see the face of my Father in Heaven."

St. Augustine captured this well when he said, "It was pride that changed angels into devils; it is humility that makes men angels," Children and angels know how to delight and how to rejoice!

In the midst of our busy lives, I fear that we have lost the art of delighting and rejoicing. How often do we focus on our disappointments, rather than on our delights?

The angels invite us to become angels and messengers for one another. For what is ultimately their role –

- To be messengers, bearers of words of consolation, hope, peace, joy, protection, healing, liberation –
- To remind others of the beauty and consolation of God's presence.
- To invite us ever more deeply into the mystery of God.
- To mirror God and God's glory to others.
- To gently lead others to God.
- To gently influence us to become angels of light, healing and love to others in need of God's healing touch today.

The important thing is not the terminology, but the realization that there are such powers, powers of numerous strength and majesty, than can break in on humans. These powers stir the deepest and most awesome responses within us; they can destroy or up build, illumine or darken.

Those who do not recognise them, who persistently refuse to admit their existence, have little chance to avoid the destructive powers in the human psyche and in the universe, they are unlikely to open themselves to the angelic, and to the God who wants to live within all of the human family.

There are dimensions of life far deeper and more mysterious than most of us usually admit!

Angels are very important because they provide people with an articulation of the conviction that God is intimately involved in human life.

Angels address the loss of the depth of being of a person.

As we become a more individualistic society, we are strangely becoming more isolated because we rely on technology and science to find all the angels. Angels in art, especially, represent a soaring of the spirit, a desire to reach out.

There is much more to life than meets our eyes here and now. So much of the resurgence of angels today and this angel mania is pure sentimentality –devoid of any authentic spirituality. But some of it is not. Some it betrays our deep human longing for God, for whom our hearts are restless until they rest in him.

Section 7:

Recordings by Luk Luk Productions for the Barefoot Angel Man

Luk Luk Productions for The Barefoot Angel Man Includes P&P

No	**Title**	**Cost**
1	Create An Angel Peace Garden CD	**51.99**
2	"Come and Explore the Wonder of Angels Series") **Double CD** (Teaching Series)	**41.99**
3	*Embracing Your Inner Essence*	**20.99**
4	Your Wounded Child is your Teacher	**20.99**
5	Communicating with angels	**20.99**
6	Heal Yourself with the Christ Energy.	**20.99**
7	Angel Healing Series 4 healing meditations **Double CD**	**31.99**
8	Heal Yourself with Angelic Love & Light."	**20.99**
9.	Four Seasons healing Meditations	**20.99**
10 & 11	Relaxation Series (Video and CD Rom	**24.99**
12 & 13	Walking with Angels CD Rom and Video	**24.99**
14	Angel healing Day CD	**20.99**
15	Therapeutic Channelling Using Touch (1 hour Video) **NEW**	**24.99**
16	Festival of Angels Video	**24.99**
17	The Barefoot Angel Man	**24.99**
18	Celebrating the Christ energies for 2012	**24.99**

Section 8 Publications by Sean, the Barefoot Angel Man.

See beginning of book.....

Section 9: Useful Contacts –friends of the Academy

Friends of Therapeutic Pathways Consultancy

Here are a few links we think you might find useful ... if you have a relevant site that we could share reciprocal links with, please let us know!

United Kingdom

- **Storth Village & local places of interest** (sea views, local activities and amenities) www.storth.com
- **Therapeutic Counselling -"Empowering you to 'Self Heal' inner child issues."** Rob has 25 years experience in counselling, counselling supervision, mediation and critical incidence debriefing. Fully accredited & insured. Contact Rob at: 01524-762292 Or by e-mail (r.crompton@aol.com)
- **NLP Training (Private or Corporate Business Training Supervision)** - contact Sharon (Master NLP Practitioner &Trainer) Tel: 015395-62625. Or e-mail Sharon at Sharon.newey@btinternet.com
- **The International Fellowship of Healers (UK)** Contact: President Gordon L. Bagshaw on 0845-2261081. www.healeasy.org.uk E-mail: healeasyorg@yahoo.co.uk
- Ty Main Duw - Poor Clare Colettine Community - Ty Mam Duw was founded in 1928 from the Notting Hill Poor Clares. This website is a wonderful look into their daily lives and beliefs, brought together with some exceptional pictures! Sisters Agatha and Damian have developed a new range of holistic products lotions and herbal ointments. The Sisters break their sleep from 11pm -1am each night to pray for us. (www.poorclarestmd.org)
- **Every Day Angels** www.everydayangelsart.com E-Mail everydayangels@btinternet.com
- **Reiki Questions** - A free Reiki answering service for professionals and individuals interested in learning more about Reiki. www.reiki-questions.com Email helen@reiki-questions.com
- **Adrain Holland Reiki Karuna Teacher and Artist** Contact **www.amazola.com**
- **The Ostra series of Books** by Carol Snell to help raise money for the Rainbow Trust for children with special needs and protection of the ancient woodlands. Contact Carol: e-mail carolesnell@yahoo.co.uk
- **The Infinite Rainbow Therapy Centre** -The charity aims to raise sufficient funds to build a center where everyone regardless of physical ability will be able to access the alternative therapies they personally need. Bringing to them understanding of self and to be the bridge of healing with gentleness, love and compassion. For those who cannot attend in person we intend to develop our out reach facilities, telephone and internet support lines, so that no one need ever feel alone. If we cannot as a charity offer support, we will be linked to as many support groups as possible that can provide alternative help. Contact Carole: carolesnell@yahoo.co.uk or Vivienne v.bell@messages.co.uk
- **Inspirational Poems** - Channelled by the Angelic Realms for living in the world today, to lift and inspire you Contact Hilary on 0114-286-4572. E-mail smee@insheff.Freeserve.co.uk
- **Channelled Paintings with specific angelic messages** - Channelled through Krysia. Contact Tel 0114-236-8702
- **Angelic Blessings** - Invitations for Weddings, cards for special occasions -special occasions and seating plans to your own personal choice. Contact: Maria on: 07976-4847401
- **Stained glass angels by Lorraine** All shapes and sizes of delightful 'hanging

angels' made with love and light for your home, quiet room or as a special gift for friends. Contact Lorraine on: 01942-671046

- **The Holistic Centre** - www.the-holistic-centre.co.uk
- **The Armana Centre** - contact Jeanne on Tel: 07967 868823.
- **The Earth Angels Shop (Sheffield)** - Website www.earth-angels.co.uk.
- **Ceramic figurines of Angels & Fairies**. rhopewell@freeuk.com
- **Electro-Magnetic Therapy** E-mail: Joan or Steve on: steve@moscompmed.co.uk or joan@moscompmed.co.uk
- **Adelphia Essential Oils** Barbara & Helen provide a range of therapies. They can be contacted on Tel: +0044 - 1942-878775 or by E-mail: barbara@adelphiaholistics.co.uk
- **Healing Today Magazine** www.nfsh.org.uk
- **Aromatic Zone** - bluebellpetlamb@ukonline.co.uk
- **Luk Luk TV Productions**: Jimmynews@talk21.com
- Okapia www.okapia.org
- Give Youth A Hand. Reg. Charity (No: 1096250 civilised society. frances@giveyouthahand.co.uk
- Monastery of St Francis and Gorton Trust. The restoration of Gorton Monastery and the Angels project clearly compliments the agendas of many local, regional and national policies & programmes covering Tourism, education, health, regeneration and Heritage priorities. If you would like to support this unique project, please Tel: +00-161-223-3211 or 01565-723838. E-mail: elaine@theangelsmanchester.com or visit their Website at: www.gortonmonastery.co.uk
- **Pilgrims Mind Body Spirit Superstore**,. www.pilgrimsmindbodyspirit.co.uk
- UK Mind Body Spirit (www.ukmindbodyspirit.com)
- **The Dogs Trust**,- www.dogstrust.org.uk
- **The Angel Diary** angeldiary@ntlworld.com
- **The Letter Manager**: www.theletterrmanager.com
- Angel Gift Store: www.angelgiftstore.com.
- www.hypnosisaudio.com
- **HigherHeart.com**: www.higherheart.com

Ireland

- **Angels At Play** - established in January 2002 by Grainne Tyndall who lives in Dublin, Ireland. website: www.angelsplay.net You can contact Grainne on Tel:

00353-863859599 or e-mail gratyndall@iolfree.ie

The LauraLynn Foundation - is a registered Charity established in Dublin, Ireland to create a hospice for terminally ill children. Set up by Jane who lost both children to cancer. Send donations to: LauraLynn Children's Hospice Foundation, National Irish Bank, Main Street, Blanchardstown, Dublin D7. Sort Code: 95 15 02. A/c: 01087029

The Angel Shop - St Michaels Shopping Centre DunLaoighre, Co Dublin, Ireland. A beautiful shop established by Mairaid who was inspired by the Archangel Michael to set up one of Ireland's finest shops dedicated to raising awareness about angels and all products associated with Angels. Email: maireadconlon@hotmail.com

Special People.

People come into your life for a reason, a season, or a lifetime.
When you figure out which it is, you know exactly what to do.
When someone is in your life for a REASON it is usually to meet a need you have expressed outwardly or inwardly.
They have come to assist you through a difficulty, to provide you with guidance and support, to aid you physically, emotionally, or spiritually.
They may seem like a godsend, and they are.
They are there for the reason you need to be.
Then, without any wrongdoing on your part or at an inconvenient time, this person will say or do something to bring the relationship to an end.
Sometimes they die. Sometimes they walk away.
Sometimes they act up or out and force you to take a stand.
What we must realize is that our need has been met, our desire fulfilled; their work is done.
The prayer you sent up has been answered and it is now time to move on.
When people come into your life for a SEASON, it is because your turn has come to share, grow, or learn.
They may bring you an experience of peace or make you laugh.
They may teach you something you have never done.
They usually give you an unbelievable amount of joy.
Believe it! It is real! But, only for a season.
LIFETIME relationships teach you lifetime lessons;
Those things you must build upon in order to have a solid emotional foundation.
Your job is to accept the lesson, love the person / people (anyway);
And put what you have learned to use in all other relationships and areas of your life.
It is said that love is blind but friendship is clairvoyant.
Thank you for being a part of my life``.

A BLESSING

May the light of your soul guide you.
May the light of your soul
Bless the work you do with secret love
And warmth of your heart.
May you see in what you do?
The beauty of your own soul.
May the sacredness of your work bring healing?
Light and renewal to those who work with you,
And those who see and receive your work.
May your work never weary you?
May it release within you wellsprings of refreshment,
Inspiration and excitement.
May you be present in what you do?
May you never become lost in the bland absences?
May the day never burden?
May the dawn find you awake and alert?
Approaching your new day with dreams,
Possibilities and promises.
May evening find you gracious and fulfilled?
May you go into the night blessed, sheltered and protected?
May your calm, console and renew YOU.

How to contact Sean:

Sean Bradley Academy

Chapel Gap,
Storth Road,
Storth,
Milnthorpe,
Cumbria.
LA7 7JL

Tel: 01524-762292

Website www.sean-bradley.com

e-mail:seansacademy@aol.com

Bibliography / References

Bradley Sean James, Angelic Energies (Publish America)
Bradley Sean James, Create An Oasis for Angels (Publish America)
Brandon, Michael.
Szekely Edmond Bordeaux, The Teachings of the Essenes from Enoch to the Dead Sea Scrolls (C.W.Daniel Publishers)

Who will separate us from the love of Christ? Will affliction, or distress, or persecution, or hunger, or nakedness, or peril, or the sword? Yet, in all this we are conquerors, through him who has granted us his love.

Romans 8:35-37